THE
CRAFTY CAT
WORKBASKET

Julie Hasler

A DAVID & CHARLES CRAFT BOOK

To Joyce Freel for her great dedication and loyalty over the years in
producing beautiful needlework for all of my books.
Happy retirement!

My thanks go to: Cara Ackerman, of Dunlicraft, for her prompt and
efficient help with the supply of materials; Valerie Janitch for her
detailed editing; Joyce Freel for her skill in sewing up the items;
Steve Matthews for his help in preparing the manuscript;
and my Mum for all her patience and support.

Photography by Di Lewis
Additional photography by Jonathon Bosley

British Library Cataloguing in Publication Data
Hasler, Julie
  The crafty cat workbasket
  I. Title
  746.1

  ISBN 0-7153-9497-5 H/B
  ISBN 0-7153-0291-4 P/B

First published 1991
Reprinted 1992
First published in paperback 1995

Printed in Italy by LEGO S.p.A
for David & Charles plc
Brunel House   Newton Abbot   Devon

CONTENTS

INTRODUCTION

There are cats stalking, climbing, snuggling, snoozing and strolling through this book. And many more that just sit and gaze at you with enormous, deeply thoughtful eyes. There are appliqué cats, quilted cats, patchwork cats, collage cats and blackwork cats: there's an abundance of cross-stitch cats, and quite a few needlepoint ones too. There are coy cats, contemplative cats, caring cats, cosy cats, cushioned cats, cartoon cats and kitchen cats. And more that aren't quite cats yet: only kittens. But unlike the cat that walked alone, they have one thing in common: they are all crafty cats.

As long as you have a basic knowledge of needlework, you can reproduce them on cushions, bags, trays, pictures, a child's cot quilt, a roller blind, a doorstop, bell pull, lavender sachets, a lacy table runner, a footstool and workbox, or a complete set of table linen and kitchen accessories. All the crafts are clearly explained, so that if you haven't experimented with them before, you will have no difficulty making up any of the items shown in the photographs. There are step-by-step instructions, accompanied by clear patterns and diagrams, describing every stage of the embroidery and making up.

Each design is shown as a specific project: many are extremely practical, others prettily decorative. But for the reader who wants to use the cat patterns and charts for other purposes, they are all so readily adaptable that the potential is almost endless. You can even adjust the size to suit yourself. So don't forget, as you turn the pages, that you can chop and change, mix and match, from craft to craft, and cat to cat. The results could be even *more* satisfying, because they will reflect your own personality in a truly unique way.

Here is a spectacular collection of ideas giving all cat-loving craftspeople the opportunity to indulge both their passions – in the production of a wide variety of designs with which to decorate their home or make gifts to delight their family and friends.

MATERIALS, EQUIPMENT AND METHODS

FABRICS
Dressmaking, furnishing and embroidery fabrics are used for the various projects. All are clearly described within the appropriate sections, together with full details of the type and amount required for each specific item.

THREADS
Use your favourite brand of regular sewing thread to make up the projects. The embroidery, cross-stitch and needle-point designs are all worked with DMC six-stranded cottons or tapestry wools.

SEWING EQUIPMENT
The usual pins, needles, scissors, tape measure and similar equipment in your sewing basket will suffice for most of the items – and a sewing machine, whilst not essential, will speed up many operations considerably. But do make sure all your equipment is in good condition: so much enjoyment is lost when you have to battle with bent pins, blunt needles and scissors that are not as sharp as they should be.

Scissors are one of your most important accessories: you'll need a large pair of special cutting out scissors, and another pair of small, pointed embroidery scissors. A third pair, reserved for paper, will prevent blunting your others cutting patterns, etc.

For much of the work, you will need tapestry needles: the size will be determined by the purpose for which they are being used. This information is given in the relevant sections.

FILLING MATERIALS
Kapok is a natural filling, and although it makes a very soft stuffing, take care to remove any stray bits of the original plant, as they can spoil the effect of your finished project. Kapok does not survive washing very well. (It also makes you sneeze!) A man-made washable polyester filling material is usually preferable, as it overcomes all these problems, and also tends to be more resilient.

GLUES AND ADHESIVES
An all-purpose clear adhesive is occasionally useful for fixing fabrics, etc. Masking tape is called for when you are mounting your embroidered pictures, but it has many other uses, too: so it is worthwhile having a roll to hand. Other tapes are mentioned where they may be found helpful.

HOOP AND FRAMES
These are advisable for cross-stitch embroidery and needlepoint. Full details of what to buy, and how to use them, are included in Sections 2 and 4.

PATTERN-MAKING EQUIPMENT
When you need to trace a pattern, use ordinary household greaseproof paper. It is not only much cheaper than proper tracing paper, but much easier to pin to your fabric and cut around accurately. When tracing designs for embroidery (when you will be stitching through the paper), use good quality white tissue paper if you have it: otherwise household greaseproof, as above.

An ordinary pencil (HB) is best for your tracings, but a light-coloured pencil will be useful for marking designs on fabrics. A softer lead pencil (2B) is helpful when you are transferring tracings to card to make a template (see below), but take care that the blacker lead doesn't smudge onto your fabric. Always *rule* straight lines.

TRANSFERRING DESIGNS

When you have traced a design and wish to transfer it to your fabric (or perhaps to a piece of card, in order to cut a template), there are several ways to do so. Choose the method which is most suited to your materials and purpose.

Tacking Method: Pin the traced design in position on the right side of your fabric. Tack along all the lines of the design through the paper with small running stitches.

Then carefully tear away the tracing paper: if you scratch the paper with the point of your needle along the lines that have been perforated by your stitches, you will find it easier to release the paper without disturbing the design.

Perforated Pattern Method: Prick all the traced lines with a needle at approximately 2mm ($\frac{1}{16}$in) intervals, or stitch along them with an unthreaded sewing machine. Rub the underside of the tracing paper with fine emery paper to remove the rough edge of the holes.

Pin the perforated paper in position on the right side of the fabric. Then gently rub pouncing paper over the surface, so that it leaves a dotted line on the fabric beneath. Remove the tracing carefully and draw over the dotted lines with a light-coloured pencil, a hard lead pencil, a dressmaker's chalk pencil or a vanishing marker.

Tracing-Through Method: If you are working on a very lightweight, light-coloured fabric, like a cotton poplin, you can sometimes trace through the fabric itself. First trace the design in the usual way, but use a black felt pen to make a really bold outline. Now place a sheet of white paper under your tracing, and place the fabric on top. Trace lightly with an ordinary lead pencil, or a light-coloured pencil.

Placing the design over a sheet of glass with a light behind it will make the tracing much clearer: a sunlit window can take the place of a proper 'light box' if you haven't access to such a piece of equipment.

Making a Template: If you need to trace a design onto a piece of card in order to cut a template, trace it first onto tracing paper in the usual way. Then draw over the lines on the *back* of the paper with a soft pencil. Now place the tracing, right side up, on your piece of card, and once again draw over the traced lines, but this time with a hard point like a ballpoint pen, a fine skewer or a knitting needle. When you remove your tracing paper, you will find the design has transferred to the card. Draw over the outline again before cutting it out.

This method *can* be used to transfer a design to light-coloured fabrics: but there is the danger of the soft black lead leaving dirty smudges on the fabric. If you want to transfer a design in this way, the safest method is to do it *in reverse* on the *back* of the fabric.

ENLARGING THE PATTERNS

Some of the patterns are too large to fit on the page. When this happens, the pattern has been reduced over a grid, so that you can enlarge it again to the correct size. Each square on the grid represents 2.5cm (1in), so you will require graph paper of that scale. Graph paper, marked with grids of various sizes, is available from stationers or stores which stock dressmaking requirements. If you are working to a metric measure, you will find it helpful to rule lines in another colour, dividing the graph paper into 2.5cm squares.

To transfer the pattern onto the graph paper, simply redraw it over the larger squares, following each line and shape exactly from square to square. You may find it helps to make a dot every time the line of the pattern crosses a line on the graph paper: then carefully draw a straight or curved line, corresponding to the original, connecting the dots.

If you plan to adapt the pattern for another purpose, you can make it any size you wish, simply by drawing it over a larger or smaller grid. To calculate the scale you will need, decide the width you want your pattern to be: then rule a horizontal line to that measurement on your graph paper. Mark this line so that it is equally divided into the same number of squares as on the original diagram. Then rule a grid over your graph paper, making the appropriate number of vertical squares to correspond with the original.

You will find it easier to pin your pattern to the fabric if you make a thinner version of your enlargement. Trace your graph paper outline onto ordinary household greaseproof paper, as described above.

It is very important to reproduce the pattern as accurately as possible. So work slowly, whether you are enlarging over a grid or just tracing an actual size drawing, as patience and care at this stage will be reflected in the finished article.

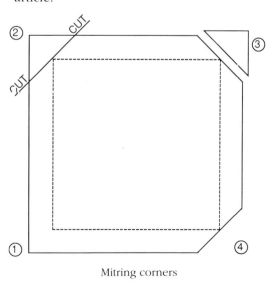

Mitring corners

MITRED CORNERS

To avoid bulky corners when turning over a double hem around a piece of fabric, cut the corner off diagonally, close to, but not quite touching, the point where the actual corner of the finished item will be (see diagram: broken line represents completed size of fabric square). Then fold the hem over neatly and stitch.

Trim off the corners in exactly the same way when you are directed to 'clip the corners', before turning two joined pieces of fabric to the right side.

USEFUL TIPS FOR A PROFESSIONAL FINISH

These points are specially important in cross-stitch embroidery, but are also generally applicable to all embroidery.

When you are stitching, it is important not to pull the fabric out of shape. To ensure that this doesn't happen, work each stitch by pushing your needle straight up through the fabric, and then straight down again, keeping the fabric smooth and taut. There should be no slack, but don't pull the thread *too* tight: draw it through so that it lies snug and flat. If your thread becomes twisted while you are working, drop the needle and let it hang down freely. It will then untwist itself. Don't continue working with twisted thread, as it will appear thinner, and won't cover your fabric satisfactorily.

Never leave your needle in the design area of your work when not in use. Not only might it distort the fabric, but no matter how good the needle, it could rust, and leave a permanent mark.

Don't carry threads across the back of an open expanse of fabric. If you are working separate areas of the same colour, finish off and begin again. Loose threads, especially dark colours, will be visible from the right side of your work when the project is finished.

PRESSING YOUR WORK

When you have completed your cross-stitch or other embroidery it will need to be pressed. Place the fabric right side down on a smooth, softly padded surface, then cover the back with a thin, damp cloth before pressing carefully and gently.

MEASUREMENTS
Both metric and imperial measurements are given for all the projects. Use one or the other, but not both, as the conversions are not accurate: instead, the designs are calculated individually, to give you the convenience of working with straightforward amounts.

ADVICE ON CLEANING EMBROIDERY
Cross-stitch projects
Cross-stitch embroideries worked on cotton or linen fabrics may be laundered quite safely, if handled with care. The following advice is recommended by DMC for the treatment of work using their stranded embroidery cotton. Always wash embroidery separately from your other laundry.

Needlepoint Projects
If you take good care of your needlepoint projects, they shouldn't need cleaning very often. However, when an item has become dirty over the years, it may be carefully hand-washed, or else dry-cleaned. If you have not used the recommended wools, be sure to check to see whether the yarns that you *have* used carry any special washing or dry-cleaning instructions. Also, make sure that your backing fabric is colour-fast.

Use warm water and a mild soap for washing. It is a good idea to do it in the bath, as this will enable you to lay the needlepoint flat in the soapy water without any creases or folds. Place the embroidery face down in the soapy water, then very gently dab the back all over with a sponge or a soft cloth: never rub, because this could loosen the threads. Continue in this way, changing the water frequently until it becomes clear.

When rinsing, never wring the needlepoint, as this can damage it. When you have finished rinsing, allow the water to drain away, then soak up the remainder with a clean, dry sponge, and allow to dry.

The needlepoint will need to be stretched again after washing.

RECOMMENDED WASHING	
Cotton or linen fabrics	**Synthetic fabrics**
Wash in soapy, warm water. Rinse thoroughly. Squeeze without twisting and hang to dry. Iron on reverse side using two layers of white linen.	NOT RECOMMENDED
BLEACHING OR WHITENING AGENT	
Product should be diluted according to manufacturer's instructions. The embroidery should be pre-soaked in clear water first, then soaked for 5 minutes in a solution of about one tablespoon of disinfectant per quart of cold water. Rinse thoroughly in cold water.	These instructions are recommended if the white of the fabric is not of a high standard of quality. If the fabric is a pure white (white with a bluish tinge) do not use bleaching and whitening agent.
DRY CLEANING	
Avoid dry cleaning. Some spot removers (benzine, trichlorethylene) can be used for an occasional small stain.	NOT RECOMMENDED even for occasional small stains.

1

NEEDLEWORK PROJECTS

KITCHEN CHAIR PAD

Paw marks on a kitchen chair usually mean mud... But these prints – which were obviously made by a Very Big Cat – are perfectly clean black cotton poplin appliquéd onto the bright red chintz. So it's quite safe to sit down! Match the ground fabric to the colour scheme of your own kitchen.

The following instructions are for a pad to fit a standard size kitchen chair. To check that it will fit your own chair, make a paper template of the seat and, if it differs in size or shape, use that as a pattern to cut your fabric.

MATERIALS

Two 38 x 35cm (15 x 14in) pieces of red chintz or similar fabric
Small piece (or scraps) of black cotton poplin or similar fabric
for the paw motifs
One 38 x 35cm (15 x 14in) piece of washable wadding
(thickness as required)
Iron-on Vilene or Pellon, or Vilene Bondaweb or Wunder-Under
(or similar single or double-sided fusing material: see step 2)
2.5m (2¾yd) black bias binding
Black sewing thread

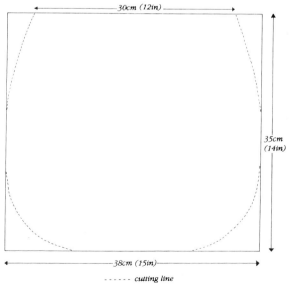

30cm (12in)

35cm
(14in)

38cm (15in)

- - - - - - *cutting line*

Cutting the fabric to shape

1 Cut the two pieces of coloured fabric to shape as shown in the diagram.
2 Appliqué the cat paw motifs (p13) onto one piece of fabric by one or other of the appliqué methods given oveleaf. (In this case, the pattern itself needs to be reversed for the two left feet: so the finished motifs for these will be correct if you *don't* reverse your tracings for the paws.) If using new fabric, make sure it is pre-shrunk. When making practical items which will require laundering try, if possible, to cut your appliqué motifs with the grain running in the same direction as the background.
3 Tack the wadding to the wrong side of the second piece of coloured fabric, then cut the wadding level with the edge of the fabric.
4 Place the appliquéd fabric on top of the other piece, wrong sides together

CUT-EDGE OR RAW-EDGE APPLIQUÉ

a) Trace the pattern for each motif, *in reverse*, onto the paper side of the Vilene/Pellon or Bondaweb/Wunder-Under.

b) Iron the Bondaweb/Wunder-Under onto the wrong side of the appliqué fabric.

c) Using small, sharp scissors, carefully cut out all the shapes. When cool, peel off the backing paper.

d) Position the motifs on the background fabric, either following the photograph or as you wish. Tack lightly into place.

e) Cover the motifs with a damp cloth and then bond them securely to the background fabric with a hot iron.

f) Stitch neatly all round the cut edge, either covering it completely with satin stitch worked by machine or hand – or using a decorative stitch such as blanket stitch, chain stitch or herringbone stitch: alternatively use an open stitch like buttonhole stitch or a machined zig-zag.

g) Remove all the tacking threads.

h) Place the work right side down on a soft, smooth surface, and press the back of the appliqué carefully.

TURNED-EDGE OR BLIND APPLIQUÉ

i) Either trace paper patterns for each motif and pin them, *in reverse*, to the Vilene/Pellon: or trace the patterns, *in reverse*, directly onto the Vilene/Pellon or Bondaweb/Wunder-Under..

ii) Cut out all the pieces very carefully and iron them onto the wrong side of the appliqué fabric, leaving at least 2.5cm (1in) between them.

iii) Using small, sharp scissors, carefully cut out all the shapes, about 5mm($\frac{1}{4}$in) beyond the edge of the Vilene/Pellon or Bondaweb/Wunder-Under. Peel the backing paper off the Bondaweb/Wunder-Under.

iv) Turn the surplus fabric neatly over the cut edge of the bonded shape, clipping where necessary, and tack to hold it exactly in place.

v) Position the motifs on the background fabric, either following the photograph or as you wish. Tack lightly into place. If using Bondaweb/Wunder-Under, cover the motifs with a damp cloth and then bond them securely to the background fabric with a hot iron.

vi) Slip-stitch neatly by hand all round the edge, using matching sewing thread and taking tiny stitches so that they show as little as possible on the right side.

vii) Remove all the tacking threads.

viii) Place the work right side down on a soft, smooth surface, and press the back of the appliqué carefully.

APPLYING BIAS BINDING

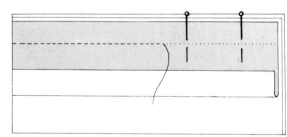

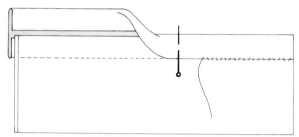

1 Open one folded edge of the bias binding and, with the right side of the binding facing the right side of your work, pin the binding to the fabric so that the cut edges are level. Stitch along the fold line of the binding by hand or machine

2 Re-fold the binding along the stitched line and press. Then turn it over the raw edge of the fabric, so that the second fold meets the stitched line on the wrong side of the work, pin the binding to the fabric so that the cut edges are level. Stitch along the fold line of the binding by hand or machine

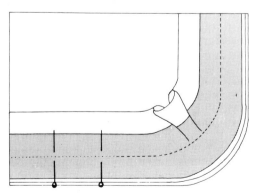

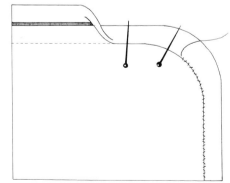

3 To bind around curved corners, apply the bias binding to the edge of your fabric as already described, but gently stretch it as you round the corner. Then stitch along the fold-line as before

4 Press, turn, pin and slip-stitch the folded edge as diagram 2: the bias cut allows the stretched binding to mould smoothly over the curved edge

with the wadding between: tack, then
join all round the edge, either by hand or
machine.
5 Trim the edges neatly, about 5mm
(¼in) from the stitching line.
6 Bind all round the trimmed edge with
bias binding (see diagrams, p12).

7 Cut two lengths of binding
(30–50cm/12–18in, as required) for the
ties. Fold each piece in half lengthways
and either oversew the side edges
together, or machine-stitch close to the
edge. Stitch the centre of each tie very
securely to the top corners of the pad.

Cat paw motif

Matching table linen and kitchen accessories: appliquéd tablecloth, serviettes, quilted placemats, tea cosy, tea towel, oven glove and pinafore (see pp16-21)

MATCHING TABLE LINEN
and Kitchen Accessories

In boldly contrasted ivory and black, this striking set of table linen is appliquéd with sleeping cat motifs, and accessories.
The tablecloth is black poplin, but the contrasting serviettes, quilted placemats, tea cosy and oven glove, and the tea towel and apron, are all in quaker cloth. This recently introduced evenweave fabric has 28 threads to the inch (2.5cm), and combines 55% linen with 45% cotton. Quaker cloth, which is also ideal for all counted thread work, is available in white and natural as well as the ivory used for these projects.

TABLECLOTH
(Finished size: 111cm/43½in square)

MATERIALS:
1.15m (1¼yd) black cotton poplin, 115cm (45in) wide
20cm (¼yd) ivory white cotton poplin, 90cm (36in) wide
(or a piece 15cm/6in x 60cm/24in wide)
20cm iron-on Vilene or Pellon, or Vilene Bondaweb or Wunder-Under
(or similar single or double-sided fusing material: see step 3)
DMC stranded cotton in black (310)
Sewing thread to match both fabrics

Tableware motif

1 Check to ensure the poplin is exactly 115cm (45in) square.

2 Mitre the corners of the tablecloth to allow for a total hem of 2cm (¾in) (see Methods section). Then make a double hem all round, first turning the raw edge under 5mm (¼in), and then turning up another 1.5cm (½in): tack and then stitch, either by hand or machine.

3 Prepare four appliqué cat motifs from the ivory white poplin, using the method that you prefer: Cut-edge or Turned-edge, as described for the previous project (Kitchen Chair Pad – step 2.) For cut-edge, work through steps a, b and c, or for turned-edge, work through steps i, ii, iii and iv: then return to this page to embroider the motifs.

4 To embroider each cat, trace the pattern onto good quality tissue or household greaseproof paper, then pin the tracing to your fabric shape, exactly matching the outer line to the edge of the fabric. Now stitch through all the inner lines indicating the cat's features, etc, with very small running stitches using black sewing thread. Then tear away the tracing paper very carefully and embroider over all the marked lines in stem stitch, using two strands of DMC cotton.

5 Pin and then tack the cats into position diagonally across each corner of the tablecloth, about 3cm (just over an inch) away from the outside edges. If using Bondaweb/Wunder-Under, cover the motifs with a damp cloth and then bond them securely to the background fabric with a hot iron.

6 Return to the Kitchen Chair Pad (previous project) to complete the appliqué: follow steps f, g and h or vi, vii and viii.

SERVIETTES

(Finished size: 30cm/11¾in square)

MATERIALS (for each serviette)

A 33cm (13in) square of ivory quaker cloth
A 15cm (6in) square of black cotton poplin for the cat motif
DMC stranded cotton in Ecru (7451)
Sewing thread to match both fabrics

1 Prepare for the hemstitched drawn threadwork border decoration all round the serviette by drawing out one single thread 1.5cm (⅝in) above each cut edge: using sharp, pointed scissors, snip these threads at the corners where they cross, then carefully draw them out with the help of a tapestry needle.

2 After drawing the threads, press the raw edge under and then press the hem up so that the top edge is one fabric thread from the bottom of the prepared border.

3 Mitre the corners, then pin and tack the hem into place before stitching by hand or machine.

4 Hemstitch the drawn threads with matching thread (see overleaf).

5 Following the directions for the appliqué cats on the tablecloth, prepare the cat motif in black poplin, embroidering it with two strands of Ecru DMC cotton: then apply it diagonally across one corner of the serviette 5mm (¼in) away from the outside edges.

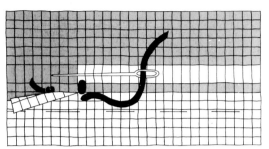

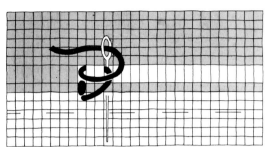

1 Bring needle up (from the wrong side) at the left edge of border and draw through until knot is securely held in hem fold. Make a small vertical stitch just to the right, catching in the hem. Now pass your needle under three vertical threads and pull together into a bundle

2 Make a small vertical stitch through the right side, emerging at the hem fold to the right of your thread needle. Continue to work in this way along the entire border

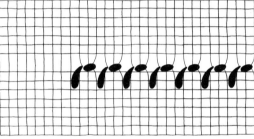

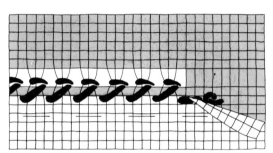

3 When the hemstitching is completed, finish off by passing the needle through both the hem fold and the hem stitches. Secure the thread and trim off any excess

4 View from right side. If you prefer the effect shown in diagram 3, work your hemstitching from the right side of the fabric: but make sure that you catch in the hem with every stitch, as it will not be visible when you are working from the right side. Finish off on the wrong side

QUILTED PLACEMATS
(Finished size: 29.5 x 40.5cm/11½ x 16in)

MATERIALS (for each placemat)

A piece of ivory quaker cloth, 29.5cm (11½in) deep x 40.5cm (16in) wide
A piece of ivory white chintz or similar cotton fabric, the same size, to back
A piece of lightweight washable wadding, the same size
A 15cm (6in) square of black cotton poplin for the cat motif
1.5m (1¾yd) black bias binding
DMC stranded cotton in Ecru (7451)
Sewing thread to match both fabrics

1 Place the wadding on the wrong side of your backing fabric, then place the quaker cloth over the wadding, right side up. Pin all three layers together, then tack and remove the pins.

2 Lightly draw on the diamond quilting pattern using a light-coloured soft pencil (or a vanishing marker) and a ruler. Machine-stitch along these lines.

3 To shape the corners, place a saucer

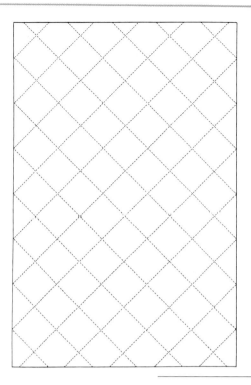

upside-down on the fabric and mark the rounded edge lightly with a soft pencil. Cut away the excess fabric, at the same time trimming the straight edges level on each side.

4 Machine-stitch all round the placemat, 5mm (¼in) from the edge. Remove all tacking stitches.

5 Following the directions for the appliqué cats on the tablecloth, prepare the cat motif in black poplin, embroidering it with two strands of Ecru DMC cotton: then apply it to the bottom right-hand corner of the placemat, 4cm (1½in) from both the lower and side edges.

6 Bind all round the edge (see previous project: Kitchen Chair Pad).

Diamond quilting pattern for the quilted placemats, tea cosy and oven glove

QUILTED TEA COSY

MATERIALS

A piece of ivory quaker cloth, 56cm (22in) deep x 33cm (13in) wide
A piece of ivory white chintz or similar cotton fabric, the same size, to line the cosy
A piece of medium-weight washable wadding, the same size
A 15cm (6in) square of black cotton poplin for the cat motif
1.5m (1¾yd) black bias binding
DMC stranded cotton in Ecru (7451)
Sewing thread to match both fabrics
Graph or squared (2.5cm/1in) paper

1 Draw up the tea cosy shape (p22) over 2.5cm (1in) squares, enlarging it from the diagram as explained in the Methods section at the beginning of the book. Then trace it onto thinner paper and cut out your pattern.

2 Place the wadding on the wrong side of your lining fabric, then place the quaker cloth over the wadding, right side up. Pin all three layers together, then tack and remove the pins.

3 Lightly draw on the diamond quilting pattern using a light-coloured soft pencil (or a vanishing marker) and a ruler.

Machine-stitch along these lines to make your quilted fabric. Remove the tacking.

4 Cut the tea cosy pattern twice from the quilted fabric.

5 Following the directions for the appliqué cats on the tablecloth, prepare the cat motif in black poplin, embroidering it with two strands of Ecru DMC cotton: then apply it to the bottom right-hand corner of one tea cosy piece, 6cm (2¼in) from both the bottom and side edges.

6 Bind the straight lower edge of both pieces (see Kitchen Chair Pad project).

7 Pin the two pieces together, wrong sides inside, and stitch all round the curved edge of the cosy, 5mm (¼in) from the cut edge.

8 Trim the edge if necessary, then bind neatly, stretching the binding around the curve.

9 To make the loop, fold a 10cm (4in) piece of bias binding in half lengthways and either oversew the long edges, or machine-stitch close to the edge. Fold in half and stitch the loop securely to the top of the cosy, turning the cut ends neatly under as you do so.

TEA TOWEL

(Finished size: 65 x 45cm/25½ x 17½in)

MATERIALS

A piece of ivory quaker cloth, 68.5cm (27in) deep x 48cm (19in) wide
Two 15cm (6in) squares of black cotton poplin for the cat motifs
DMC stranded cotton in Ecru (7451)
Sewing thread to match both fabrics

1 Prepare for the hemstitched drawn threadwork border decoration at one end of the tea towel by drawing out one horizontal thread 2.5cm (1in) above the cut edge: using sharp, pointed scissors, snip the thread and then draw it out carefully with the help of a tapestry needle.

2 After drawing the thread, press the raw edge under and then press the hem up so that the top edge is one fabric thread from the bottom of the border.

3 Pin and tack a 5mm (¼in) double hem

on all the other edges, mitring the corner, (see p7), and stitch by hand or machine. Remove the pins and tacking threads.

4 Hemstitch the drawn thread border with matching thread (see diagrams: p18)

5 Following the directions for the appliqué cats on the tablecloth, prepare two motifs in black poplin, embroidering them with two strands of Ecru DMC cotton: then apply one to each bottom corner of the tea towel, 5cm (2in) above the lower edge.

PINAFORE

MATERIALS

A 50cm (20in) square, two 50 x 5cm (20 x 2in) strips, and a 43 x 10cm (17 x 4in)
strip, all in ivory quaker cloth
A 15cm (6in) square of black cotton poplin for the cat motif
1.6m (1¾yd) black bias binding
DMC stranded cotton in Ecru (7451)
Sewing thread to match both fabrics

1 Round off the two bottom corners of the square of quaker cloth: to do this, place a tea-plate upside-down on the fabric and lightly mark a curved line around the edge with a soft pencil. Cut away the excess fabric.

2 Bind the sides and bottom edge (see previous project: Kitchen Chair Pad), leaving the top edge raw.

3 Make the ties from the two long strips of fabric: fold in and tack a 5mm (¼in) hem around the two long sides and one

short end of each strip (mitre the corners: see p7). Fold the strips in half lengthways, then either oversew the hemmed edges together by hand, or machine-stitch them close to the edge.

4 Use the remaining strip of fabric to make the waistband: fold in and tack a 5mm (¼in) hem along the two short edges. Gather the top edge of the pinafore, then pin the waistband over the gathers, right sides facing and cut edges level. Draw up the gathers to fit, distributing them evenly: tack, then stitch the waistband into position.

5 Fold the waistband over the top edge of the pinafore front: turn under the raw edge, then pin and tack into position over the gathers, level with the previous stitching line. Stitch securely by hand or machine.

6 Insert the raw edges of the ties at least 1cm (⅜in) into the open ends of the waistband: pin and tack to hold in place, then stitch very securely.

7 Remove all tacking stitches.

8 Following the directions for the appliqué cats on the tablecloth, prepare cat motif in black poplin, embroidering it with two strands of Ecru DMC cotton: then apply it to the bottom right-hand corner of the pinafore, 5cm (2in) from both the lower and side edges.

QUILTED OVEN GLOVE

MATERIALS

A piece of ivory quaker cloth, 35.5cm (14in) deep x 46cm (18in) wide
A piece of ivory white chintz or similar cotton fabric, the same size, to line the glove
A piece of lightweight washable wadding, the same size
A 15cm (6in) square of black cotton poplin for the cat motif
70cm (¾yd) black bias binding
DMC stranded cotton in Ecru (7451)
Sewing thread to match both fabrics
Graph or squared (2.5cm/1in) paper

1 Draw up the oven glove shape (p23) over 2.5cm (1in) squares, enlarging it as explained in the Methods section. Then trace it onto thinner paper and cut out your pattern. (A 5mm/¼in seam allowance is included.)

2 Place the wadding on the wrong side of your lining fabric, then place the quaker cloth over the wadding, right side up. Pin all three layers together, then tack and remove the pins.

3 Lightly draw on the diamond quilting pattern (p19) using a light-coloured soft pencil (or a vanishing marker) and a ruler. Machine-stitch along these lines to make your quilted fabric. Remove the tacking.

4 Cut the oven glove pattern once in the quilted fabric, then reverse the pattern to cut the second piece.

5 Following the directions for the appliqué cats on the tablecloth, prepare the cat motif in black poplin, embroidering it with two strands of Ecru DMC cotton: then apply it centrally to one glove piece, 5cm (2in) above wrist edge.

6 Pin the two pieces together, right sides facing, and join all round, leaving the wrist edges open (allow a 5mm/¼in seam). Trim the raw edges neatly and then oversew them.

7 Turn to the right side and bind the raw wrist edges (see: Kitchen Chair Pad).

8 Cut a 15cm (6in) length of bias binding and make a loop to hang the glove. Fold it in half lengthways and either oversew the long edges, or machine-stitch close to the edge. Fold in half and stitch the cut end securely just inside the glove.

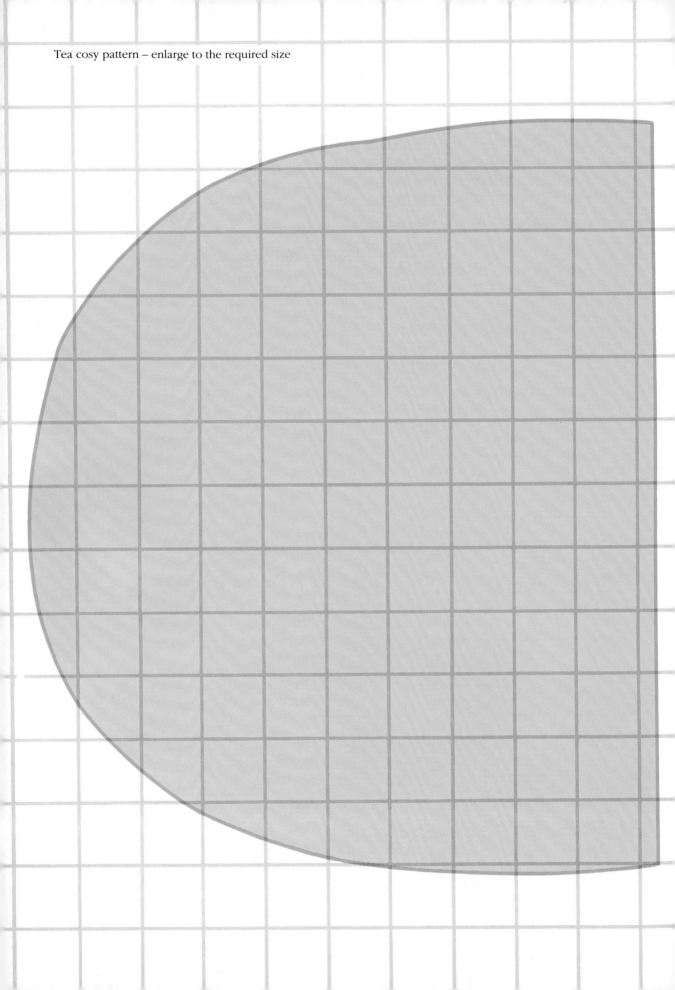

Tea cosy pattern – enlarge to the required size

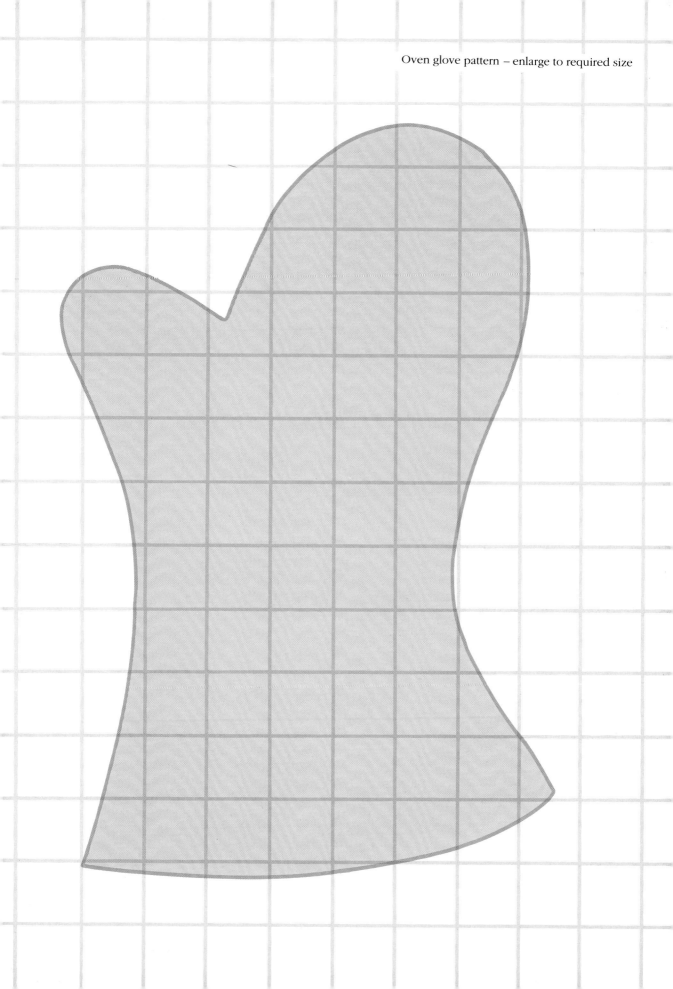

Oven glove pattern – enlarge to required size

CHILD'S COT QUILT

This beautiful satin quilt has a playful kitten trying to catch floating bubbles stitched into the cosy thickness of its soft padding. A lovely gift for a small child that will be treasured for many years to come. It is important to use a good quality satin, as inferior fabrics crease easily, spoiling the effect of the quilting: nor do they wear well. Peach is just one of the delicate shades from which to make your choice.

MATERIALS

1.5m (1⅝yd) satin (see above), 115cm (45in) wide
1.5m (1⅝yd) matching cotton sheeting, to back
1.5m(1⅝yd) medium-weight wadding, 115cm (45in) wide
Sewing thread to match the fabric
Sewing thread in a slightly darker shade for the quilting
Graph or squared (2.5cm/1in) paper

(Finished size: 132 x 101.5cm/52 x 40in)

1 Cut the following pieces of satin:
One piece 114 x 84cm (45 x 33in) for the centre
Two pieces 134 x 12cm (53½ x 5in) for the sides
Two pieces 12 x 84cm (5 x 33in) for the ends
(These pieces include a 1cm/⅜in seam allowance)

2 Pin the two end pieces to the top and bottom of the centre panel, right sides facing, and cut edges level: stitch together, making a 1cm (⅜in) seam. Join the two side strips to the centre panel and ends in the same way. Mitre the joined corners and trim off any excess fabric, then press the seams open.

3 Draw up the kitten and bubbles design over 2.5cm (1in) squares, enlarging it from the diagram as explained in the Methods section at the beginning of the book. Then trace it onto good quality tissue paper or household greaseproof paper.

4 Transfer the design to your fabric using either the Tacking Method or the Perforated Pattern Method, as described in the same section.

5 Cut the sheeting fabric to size for the quilt back: 134 x 104cm (53½ x 41½in) (this includes a 1cm (⅜in) seam allowance).

6 Cut a piece of wadding 132 x 102cm (53 x 41in), and place it on the wrong side of the sheeting, with an equal surplus of fabric all round. Tack to hold in place.

7 Place the satin on top of the wadding, right side up, the edges of the satin and sheeting exactly level. Pin all round, through the three layers, about 2cm (¾in) from the edge.

8 Fold in and pin a 1cm (⅜in) hem all round both pieces of fabric (mitre the corners: see Methods section), then tack them together. Oversew the edges together, or machine-stitch close to the edge. Remove all pins and tacking stitches.

9 Quilt all round the central panel,

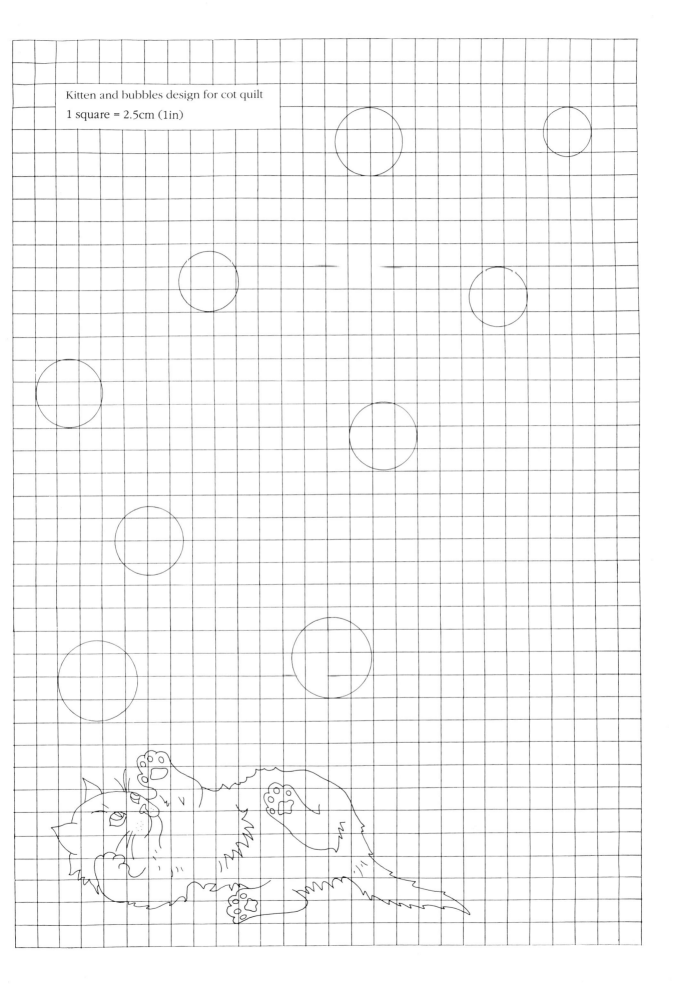

Kitten and bubbles design for cot quilt

1 square = 2.5cm (1in)

through the seam line, using a single length of thread, no more than 50cm (20in) long, in darker shade. Knot the thread, then push your needle straight down from the top, through all three layers: pull gently but firmly until the knot slips through and is held in the wadding (snip off any excess thread still visible).

Quilt with an even running stitch, about 2mm (¹⁄₁₆in) long on both sides of the work: draw the thread up so that there is no slack and it is taut enough to hold the layers of fabric and wadding firmly together without being so tight that it causes them to pucker.

To finish off the thread, make a knot close to the surface of the fabric, then push the needle through a stitch-length away and run it through the wadding for a short distance before bringing it out again and pulling the knot through so that it is held in the wadding. Cut the thread off close to the surface.

10 Quilt around the kitten and bubbles in exactly the same way, following the design very carefully and making your stitches even tinier where necessary.

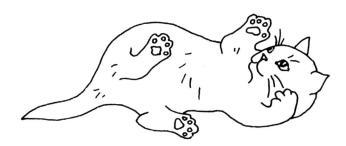

PATCHWORK KNITTING BAG

Leftover cuttings from past dressmaking could make this attractive work-bag a very economical project, as well as something that will be useful for a long time to come. The example illustrated combines three different cotton prints with a plain satin for the appliqué cat, but the choice is yours – either dependent on what fabrics you have available – or, if you are buying them specially, the mix-and-match that appeals to you. In all, you will need six strips 75cm (30in) long x 9cm (3½in) wide: two strips of each design were used for the bag in the photograph.

MATERIALS

Six strips of printed cotton
(see above), each 75cm (30in) long x 9cm (3½in) wide
A piece of cotton fabric, 75cm (30in) long x 44cm (17¼in) wide, for the lining
A piece of satin, 18cm (7in) deep x 21cm (8in) wide, for the cat motif
A piece of lightweight wadding, 60 x 42cm (24 x 16½in)
Iron-on Vilene or Pellon, 18 x 21cm (7 x 8in)
A pair of wooden bag-handles (as illustrated)
Matching sewing threads

(Measurements include a 1cm/⅜in seam allowance)

1 Allowing 1cm (⅜in) seams, machine-stitch all the strips of printed cotton fabric together lengthways, to make your patchwork. Press all the seams open.
2 Place your patchwork right side down with the wadding on top – leaving an equal amount of surplus fabric at the top and bottom, and on each side: pin and then tack together. Now place the lining fabric over the wadding, right side up, top and bottom edges level, but with the printed cotton extending equally on each side: pin and then tack together.
3 Remove the pins, then turn over and machine-stitch the printed cotton along the existing seams, leaving the sides and ends open. Remove the tacking stitches from the quilted fabric.

4 Trace the cat motif onto good quality tissue or household greaseproof paper. Iron the Vilene or Pellon onto the back of the satin, then pin the tracing on top of the satin. Hand- or machine-stitch carefully along all the traced lines. Then tear away the tracing paper and cut round the cat very close to the stitches marking the outer edge, using a sharp pair of embroidery scissors.

Pin and tack the cat into place on the quilted patchwork, positioning it centrally, with the tip of the ear approximately 18cm (7in) from the top edge. Machine or hand-stitch the motif into place as explained for Cut-Edge Appliqué (see the Kitchen Chair Pad at the beginning of this section). Remove all pins and tacking stitches.

5 Right side inside, fold your quilted fabric in half, across the patchwork strips.

6 Working from the inside of the bag, join only the printed cotton at each side, beginning at the folded bottom edge and stitching up for 20cm (8in). Press the edges of the seams back.

7 Now turn the raw side edges of the lining fabric under 1cm (³/8in): then pin and oversew these edges together by hand for 20cm (8in) from the bottom of the bag, taking care not to catch in the printed cotton.

8 Turn under a 1cm (³/8in) hem along the remaining raw side edges of the printed cotton, then pin to the side edges of the lining fabric. Either oversew together by hand, or machine-stitch close to the edge: strengthen the top of the seams joining the two sides with extra stitching.

9 Turn in the raw edges at the top of the bag and join the patchwork to the lining fabric in the same way.

10 Gather the top edges of the bag, then push them through the slots in the handles, folding them over the lining on the inside. Draw up the gathers to fit: tack, then stitch securely to the lining, just below the bottom of each handle.

Motif for patchwork bag

'ADAM AND EVE' LACE COLLAGE

An exquisite example of lace collage that should inspire you to create similar lace pictures of other subjects, suggested by the pieces of lace that you have available, or that you buy specially.

(above) The completed collage
(left) Patchwork knitting bag (see p28)

MATERIALS

Odd pieces and scraps of lace (see below)
A piece of black cotton fabric, 77cm (30in) deep x 56cm (22in) wide,
for the background
Sewing thread to match the lace

Most department stores stock a good selection of new lace in a variety of widths, though this often tends to be pure white, with only a small range in off-white or cream.

However, the deep creams, ivory or ecru tints of old lace make it particularly suitable for collage, so keep a watchful eye open for any good pieces in second-hand shops, or at jumble sales or flea markets. Old-fashioned lace collars and cuffs, dressing table sets, doilies, delicate pieces of crochet or cutwork, even net curtains, can all provide wonderful material for collage. Carefully colour-matched, and mounted on black cotton, as they are here, the effect can be quite dramatic.

On the other hand, the lace can be coloured: either lightly tinted, or using strong colours to create a bold effect. Use fabric paints or dyes, watercolours or drawing inks to tint your lace. Dampen it first and lay it on a sheet of white paper, then work very carefully, slowly applying more and more colour with a soft paintbrush, a small sponge or a piece of cotton wool, until you achieve just the shade you are aiming for.

The lace can, of course, be combined with fabric. If you find your enthusiasm extending to fabric collage, you will find it useful to iron your fabric onto lightweight Vilene or Pellon before you cut it, to prevent fraying. The pieces of fabric can then be glued to the background to build up your design.

1 Trace the cat motif, then cut it out to make a template. Pin this pattern to a piece of lace and cut the shape out very accurately with a pair of sharp scissors. Turn the template over to cut the cat in reverse, positioning it so that the design on the lace matches that on the first cat as closely as possible, to make both cats look alike.

2 The base of the tree is a piece of cutwork linen from an old dress, but an appropriately shaped piece of lace would be equally suitable. The tree trunk is a 19cm (7½in) length of lace insertion, 2cm (¾in) wide. And the leafy top of the tree is a crocheted cotton mat, 23cm (9in) in diameter. But again, this could be a circle cut from a piece of lace fabric; or it could be made up from a collection of small individual motifs.

3 When all the pieces have been prepared, place them on the background fabric and keep moving them about until you have found the most effective arrangement. Then pin them into position. Starting with the base of the tree, sew all the pieces of lace to the background fabric, using tiny running stitches close to the edge. When the tree is in position, stitch the cats into place.

4 Finally, embroider the outline of the cats evenly in stem stitch, to emphasise their smooth and shapely lines.

5 Mount and frame the collage as described at the end of Section 3 (Cross-stitch Pictures).

Motif for lace collage

WOVEN RIBBON CUSHION

Woven ribbons create a specially pretty effect, the smoothly gleaming satin catching the light in both directions. You can mix or match your colours and widths, and even weave in some fancy ribbons or lace here and there for added interest. This attractive cushion uses a panel of pink satin ribbon as a background for an appliqué cat – which is cut from the same bold cotton print that is used for the base fabric of the cushion.

MATERIALS

40cm (¹/₂yd) printed cotton, 90cm (36in) wide, for the cushion cover
30cm (12in) iron-on Vilene or Pellon, 60cm (24in) wide
11m (11¹/₂yd) single-face pink satin ribbon, 15mm (⁵/₈in) wide
A 35cm (14in) square cushion pad
Matching sewing threads

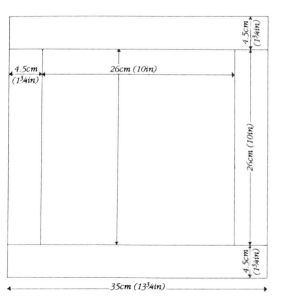

Finished dimensions of cushion (including seam allowances

1 Begin by making the woven ribbon panel as follows. Cut a 28cm (11in) square of Vilene or Pellon and place it, *bonded side up*, on your ironing cloth: pin the corners temporarily. Cut the ribbon into thirty-six 30cm (thirty-four 12in) lengths.

2 Place a length of ribbon on top of the Vilene/Pellon, the edge of the ribbon level with one vertical edge of the Vilene/Pellon square, and the ends overlapping equally at the top and bottom: pin the overlap to your ironing board, pushing the pins in at an angle, their heads away from the work.

Lay another length of ribbon alongside, almost, but not quite, touching: pin the surplus at top and bottom as before. Continue until you have pinned eighteen 30cm (seventeen 12in) strips of ribbon in the same direction, and the Vilene/Pellon is covered. Check that they are all smooth and flat, but not stretched.

3 Now weave a piece of ribbon horizontally under and over the vertical strips, positioned so that the outer edge of the ribbon is level with the top edge of the Vilene/Pellon: pin the surplus at each end.

Weave the remaining seventeen (sixteen) lengths in the same way, again with the edges close together, but not quite touching.

4 When the weaving is complete, adjust the pins to ensure that it is absolutely smooth and even. When you are satisfied, place a damp cloth over the work and press it very thoroughly to ensure the ribbon is firmly bonded to the Vilene/Pellon backing.

5 Remove the pins, turn the panel over, and fold all the surplus ends of ribbon over the edge of the Vilene/Pellon: pin them to the back and then tack to hold them in place. Press the edges of the panel to neaten.

6 Cut two 37cm (14½in) squares of printed cotton for the front and back of the cushion (these measurements include a 1cm/³⁄₈in seam allowance). Cut another piece, 26cm (10½in) square, for the cat motif.

7 Trace the cat motif (p36) onto good quality tissue or household greaseproof paper. Back the 26cm (10½in) printed cotton square with iron-on Vilene/Pellon, then pin your tracing on top. Using small tacking stitches, mark all the lines of the design within the cat shape. Then cut the motif along the outside line and tear away the remaining tracing paper very carefully.

8 Pin and tack the cat motif centrally onto your panel of woven ribbon. Then machine all round the edge, and over the design lines, using a close zig-zag stitch. Embroider the eye detail by hand in chain stitch.

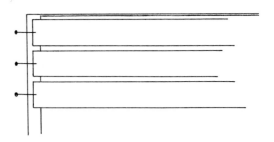

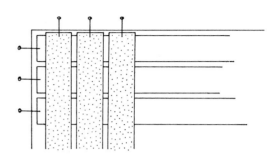

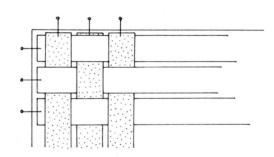

Ribbon Weaving Technique

9 Pin, and then tack, the ribbon panel to the centre of the cushion front. Slip-stitch it neatly into place all round the edge.

10 With the right sides together, join the front and back of the cushion along three sides. Clip the corners and trim the seams, then turn to the right side and fold under and tack the seam allowance along the two remaining raw edges. Press well.

11 Insert the cushion pad and slip-stitch the remaining side edges neatly together.

Appliqué motif for woven ribbon cushion

BLACKWORK ROLLER BLIND

Improve your kitchen window with this striking roller blind made from an inexpensive D-I-Y kit. The cuts are embroidered in blackwork, which is very quick and easy to do. You will need to begin by measuring your window in order to buy a self-assembly roller blind kit to fit.

MATERIALS

A piece of white Linda embroidery fabric, with 27 stitches to the inch (2.5cm):
see Step 2 for the measurements
A piece of strong black fabric slightly larger than your window
DMC stranded cotton in black (310)
Black sewing thread
A size 24 tapestry needle
A roller blind kit to fit your window
Strong adhesive (if necessary: see step 6)

1 Cut the black fabric 2cm (³⁄₄in) wider than your window, to allow for a 1cm (³⁄₈in) hem on each side. Measure round the bottom rail of your roller blind: cut the fabric the same length as the depth of your window *plus* this amount.

2 Cut a strip of Linda embroidery fabric the same width as your black fabric (2cm/³⁄₄in wider than your window), and 18cm (7in) deep (this includes a 1cm/³⁄₈in seam allowance all round).

3 Embroider the blackwork design (p38) on the white strip, using a tapestry needle and one strand of DMC cotton. Each dot on the pattern represents a hole in the fabric, and the entire design is worked in basic backstitch (see the next section). Begin at the centre and work as many repeats as necessary across the width of the fabric. Although the embroidery may be worked in the hand, if you prefer, it is usually more satisfactory to use a 15cm (6in) diameter hoop.

4 Decide the most suitable position for your embroidered strip on the blind, and cut the black fabric into two pieces to accommodate it. Turn under and tack a 1cm (³⁄₈in) hem along the two edges that you have just cut, then pin them to the top and bottom of the embroidered strip, overlapping 1cm (³⁄₈in). Tack, then either machine or hand-stitch the pieces of fabric to the embroidered strip. Remove tacking stitches.

5 Make a narrow double hem down both sides of the blind. Turn the raw bottom edge under 1cm (³⁄₈in) and tack: then turn up a hem on the wrong side, deep enough to hold the bottom rail of the fitment. Pin, then tack and machine or hand-stitch. Leave the top edge of the blind fabric raw.

6 If your roller doesn't have a self-adhesive strip, use a strong adhesive to fix the fabric into position. Take great care to ensure that the top edge of the fabric is absolutely straight on the roller, or the blind will not hang properly.

7 Slide the bottom rail through the hem at the base of the blind, oversew the ends, and then fix the pull cord at the centre.

Black work roller blind
pattern and (opposite)
the completed blind
(see p37)

2
CROSS-STITCH PROJECTS

BASIC CROSS-STITCH TECHNIQUE
Cross-stitch must be one of the most popular forms of embroidery: partly because it is so quick and easy to learn and do – and partly because it is so effective when it is finished. There are only a few simple basic rules, and once you have mastered those, you can attempt any of the designs in the book. Practice makes perfect, as with any craft: so it's wise to start with a small, simple design. But perfection in cross-stitch is soon achieved, and it won't be long before you'll have no qualms about attempting the most complex projects.

The embroidery is worked with a small blunt tapestry needle (size 24 or 26) over counted threads on an evenweave fabric. The 'even weave' is important: the fabric must have the same number of horizontal and vertical threads to the inch (2.5cm). If they differ, your design will be distorted.

Some of the most suitable cross-stitch embroidery fabrics are called Linda, Hardanger and Aida Ainring: they all come in a wide range of colours, with varying thread counts. On Linda, which is a linen woven with single threads, your crosses should cover two *threads* in each direction; on Hardanger, they cover two *blocks* of threads; and on Aida Ainring, *one block*. The more crosses to the inch (2.5cm), the smaller your stitches will be. The type of fabric used, and the number of threads or blocks (stitches) to the inch (2.5cm), is listed in the materials for each design.

Six-stranded embroidery cotton is

used, the number of strands depending on the fabric: the smaller your crosses, the fewer strands you will need. Two or three strands are the most common number: use two strands for twelve or more stitches to the inch (2.5cm), and three strands for eleven or less stitches. All the designs in the book are keyed to DMC stranded embroidery cottons, and full details of the shade and number of strands used are specified for each individual project.

A pair of small, sharp, pointed embroidery scissors is essential, especially when a mistake has to be cut out.

Although cross-stitch may be worked in the hand, it is easier to achieve a perfectly smooth and even finish if the fabric is absolutely flat, and stretched taut over a hoop. Choose a 10cm (4in), 12.5cm (5in) or 15cm (6in) diameter plastic or wooden hoop, with a screw-type tension adjuster.

PREPARING TO WORK
To prevent the fabric ravelling while you work, you can either cover the edges with a fold of masking tape, or else whip-stitch or machine-stitch over them.

Each square on the chart represents a cross-stitch worked over a square of fabric, and each symbol represents a colour. The 'square' on the fabric consists of a block formed by the vertical and horizontal threads. Each vertical and horizontal thread on the diagrams represents a *block* of threads on an Aida fabric, or *two* threads on an evenweave

linen fabric like Linda.

To make your first stitch, you will need to find the exact centrepoint of the chart: follow the arrows to the point where they intersect. Find the centre of your fabric by folding it in half vertically and then horizontally, pinching the folds (or you can mark the fold lines with basting stitches). The centre stitch of the charted design will fall where the folds in the fabric meet.

However, it is best to begin at the top of the design. So count the squares up from the centre of the chart, and then count left or right to the first symbol. Now count the corresponding number of blocks or pairs of threads up and across from the centre of the fabric – and begin at that point.

To place the fabric in the embroidery hoop, place the area to be embroidered over the inner ring and carefully push the outer ring down over it. Pull the fabric gently and evenly, making sure that it is drum taut in the hoop and that the mesh is straight, tightening the screw adjuster as you do so. When working, you will find it best to have the screw in the 'ten o'clock' position, as this will prevent your thread becoming tangled in the screw with each stitch. If you are left-handed, have the screw in the 'one o'clock' position. As you work, re-tighten the fabric to keep it taut.

Always separate the strands of cotton, and then place them together again before threading your needle and beginning to stitch. Never double the thread: use two separate strands.

BASIC CROSS-STITCH
Each cross-stitch is worked over two or more threads in each direction. In the case of an evenweave linen like Linda, which has individually woven threads, make the stitch over two vertical and two horizontal threads. Aida fabrics, like Ainring, have thinner threads woven in groups to form separate blocks: work one stitch over each block.

To begin the stitch, bring the needle up from the wrong side, through a hole in the fabric, as in figure 1, at the left end of a row of stitches of the same colour. Fasten the end of the thread by holding a short length on the underside of the fabric and securing it with the first two or three stitches made, as figure 2. Never use knots to fasten your thread, as this will create bumps on the back.

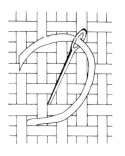

Fig 1

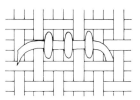

Fig 2

Now bring the needle diagonally across one square (a block or pair of threads) to the right, and push it down through the hole in the fabric as in figure 1. This is the first half of the stitch. Continue in this way until the end of the row of stitches in that colour is reached. Your stitches should be diagonal on the right side of the fabric, and vertical on the wrong side.

Complete the second half of the stitch by crossing back from right to left to form an X as in figure 3.

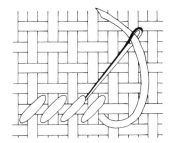

Fig 3

Work all the stitches in the row by completing the crosses as figure 4. Work vertical lines of stitches as shown in figure 5.

If you prefer to complete one stitch at a time, it makes no difference: just work each cross individually all along the row, as you would do for isolated stitches.

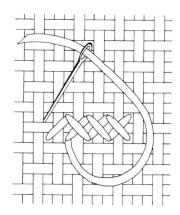

Fig 4

Fig 5

Finish off the thread by running your needle under four or more stitches on the wrong side of the work, as shown in figure 6, and then cutting it off close.

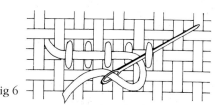

Fig 6

Note: Each vertical and horizontal thread on the diagrams represents a *block* of threads on an Aida fabric like Ainring, or a *pair of threads* on an evenweave linen like Linda

BASIC BACKSTITCH

Some of the designs are outlined with backstitch to give them greater emphasis. Backstitch is also used to pick out fine details and features.

Always work the backstitch after all the cross-stitch embroidery is finished, using one strand less than that used for the cross-stitch. For example, if three strands of cotton have been used to work the cross-stitch embroidery, use two strands for the backstitching. However, if only one strand of cotton is used to work the cross-stitch, one strand is also used for the backstitching.

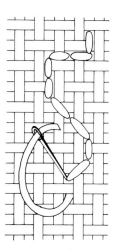

Fig 7

Backstitch is worked from hole to hole, following the same blocks as the cross-stitches, and can be stitched in vertical, horizontal or diagonal lines, as shown. Take care not to pull the stitches too tight, or the contrast of colour will be lost. Finish off the threads as for cross-stitch.

PIN CUSHION

Paw-prints cover this amusing, but useful, pin cushion. The small, simple design makes it an ideal project to start with if you have never attempted cross-stitch before (see photo on page 111).

MATERIALS

Two 11cm (4½in) squares of sky-blue Ainring embroidery fabric
with 18 stitches to the inch (2.5cm)
Small amount of kapok or polyester stuffing
DMC stranded cotton in Medium Peach (352)
Sewing thread to match fabric

1 Work the cross-stitch design from the chart, using two strands of DMC embroidery cotton.
2 Place the two squares of fabric right sides together and tack.
3 Either machine or hand-stitch together, following the edge of the design: leave about 4cm (1½in) open on one side.
4 Remove the tacking stitches, clip the corners and turn to the right side.
5 Stuff the pin cushion firmly, pushing in small amounts at a time so that it is evenly filled. Turn in the raw edges and slip-stitch the opening.

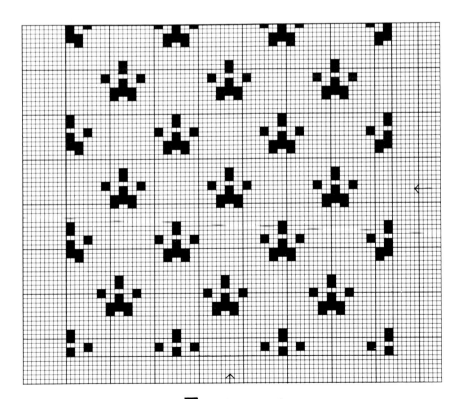

■ Medium Peach

OVAL WOODEN TRAY

This antique-style wooden tray with ornate brass handles is specially made so that you can assemble it yourself, with your embroidery mounted inside. The non-reflective glass is sealed into the wooden rim, so that any spills cannot seep through and damage the fabric underneath. The simple, single colour cross-stitch design would be another ideal project for a beginner. Such tray kits are available from various suppliers. Adjust the measurements below to fit your tray.

MATERIALS

A 27 x 40cm (10½in x 15¾in) piece of cream Ainring embroidery fabric with 18 stitches to the inch (2.5cm)
A piece of medium-weight Vilene or Pellon, the same size
A piece of Vilene Bondaweb or Wunder-Under, the same size
DMC stranded cotton in Dark Mahogany (400)
Oval wooden tray

1 Work the cross-stitch design, using two strands of DMC cotton.
2 When the embroidery is finished, stiffen the fabric by ironing it onto the Bondaweb/Wunder-Under: remove the paper backing and then iron it onto the Vilene/Pellon.
3 In your tray kit you will find a piece of thick oval board and a piece of thin oval card: place the thick oval board on a sheet of tracing paper and draw round it. Cut out this oval and use it as a pattern to cut your embroidery to size, making sure that your design is absolutely central.
4 Place the tray right side down: polish the glass with a soft cloth and check that

it is completely clear. Then fit your embroidery, right side down, over the glass – followed by the thin oval card, and then the thick oval board. This will fill the back of the frame.
5 Peel the backing off the felt base and then carefully place it over the back filling card and the wooden surround, to secure the pieces inside: the self-adhesive felt base is cut slightly smaller than the wood, to make it fit easily.
6 Lastly, press the four small brass feet into the wooden base: if you are unable to do this with your thumbs, gently *push* them in with the head of a small hammer, but avoid knocking them in, as this could disturb the glass seal.

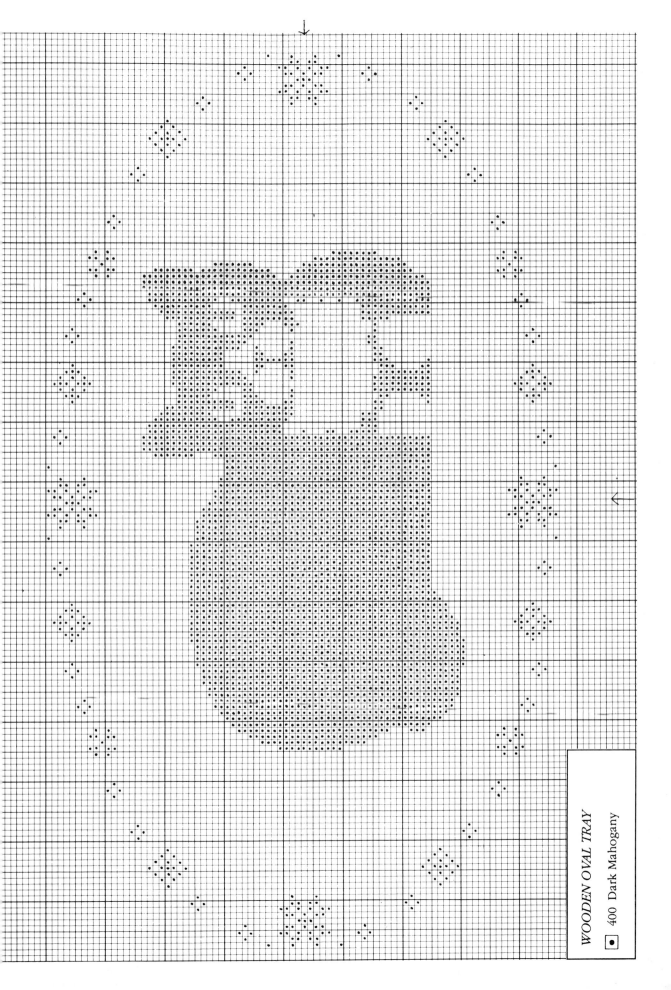

ROUND BRASS TRAY

This small (23cm/9in diameter) tray has an attractive brass edge, a solid wooden base with three rubber feet, and a glass top to protect the embroidery underneath. It is easily assembled, and would make a charming gift for any cat lover. Such tray kits are available from various suppliers. Adjust the measurements below to fit your tray.

MATERIALS

A 33cm (13in) square of sky blue Ainring embroidery fabric
with 18 stitches to the inch (2.5cm)
A 33cm (13in) square of Vilene or Pellon
A 33cm (13in) square of Vilene Bondaweb or Wunder-Under
DMC stranded cotton in the colours indicated
A 23cm (9in) diameter round tray

1 Work the cross-stitch design (pp48–9), using two strands of DMC cotton.
2 When the embroidery is finished, stiffen the fabric by ironing it onto the Bondaweb/Wunder-Under: remove the paper backing and then iron it onto the Vilene/Pellon.
3 Carefully ease the rim off the tray and set it aside.
4 Use the round piece of glass from the tray as a template to cut your fabric to size: to do this, place the glass over your embroidery and, when you are satisfied that the design is absolutely central, draw round the edge of the glass with a soft pencil.
5 Carefully cut the fabric along this line.
6 Polish the glass with a soft cloth and check that it is absolutely clear, then re-assemble the tray with the design replacing the original blank card. Hold the rim tightly against the glass and use a small hammer to tap the nails into the wood: to avoid damaging the rim, pad the hammer-head by covering it with a piece of soft material.

(left) Oval wooden tray and round brass tray with cross-stitch embroidery

ROUND BRASS TRAY

Symbol	Code	Name
⧄	503	Blue Green
◢	680	Dark Mustard
☐		White
⫾	754	Light Peach
○	3345	Dark Hunter Green
⌊	741	Medium Tangerine
⸫	3348	Light Yellow Green
⟍	504	Light Blue Green
◼	950	Medium Flesh Pink
■	310	Black
V	352	Medium Peach
◁	3347	Medium Avocado Green
+	744	Primrose Yellow
6	318	Light Grey
‖‖	729	Medium Old Gold
△	951	Light Flesh Pink
⸳	966	Pale Green
✕	3346	Dark Spring Green
—	745	Light Yellow
◤	740	Deep Orange
⧅	413	Charcoal Grey
⊟	676	Gold
⧄	677	Light Pine
·	948	Very Light Peach
●	895	Dark Evergreen
‖	742	Light Tangerine
⊋	743	Dark Yellow

Back Stitch
Outline flower 318 Light Grey
Outline eyes 310 Black
Outline butterfly 413 Charcoal
Grey

BRASS BELL PULL

An irrepressible collection of kittens climb into all kinds of mischief on an embroidered bell pull, making it an amusing and eye-catching wall decoration for any room.

MATERIALS

A piece of beige Linda embroidery fabric with 27 threads to the inch (2.5cm),
130cm (51in) deep x 23cm (9in) wide
DMC stranded embroidery cotton in the colours indicated
Sewing thread to match fabric
A pair of 20cm (8in) brass bell-pull ends

(Measurements allow for a 1cm/³⁄₈in hem all round)

1 Work the cross-stitch design (pp52–7), using two strands of DMC cotton: use one strand for the backstitch.
2 Finish off the raw edges of the fabric by machining over them with a zig-zag stitch. Then press the embroidery (see Methods section).

3 Machine-stitch a 1cm (³⁄₈in) hem all round, mitring the corners (see Methods section).
4 Fit the ends of the fabric through the bell-pull pieces, and machine-stitch into place.

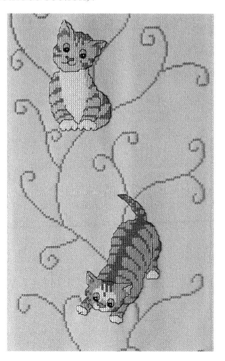

(left) The completed brass and cross-stitch bell pull and (above) a detail of the embroidery

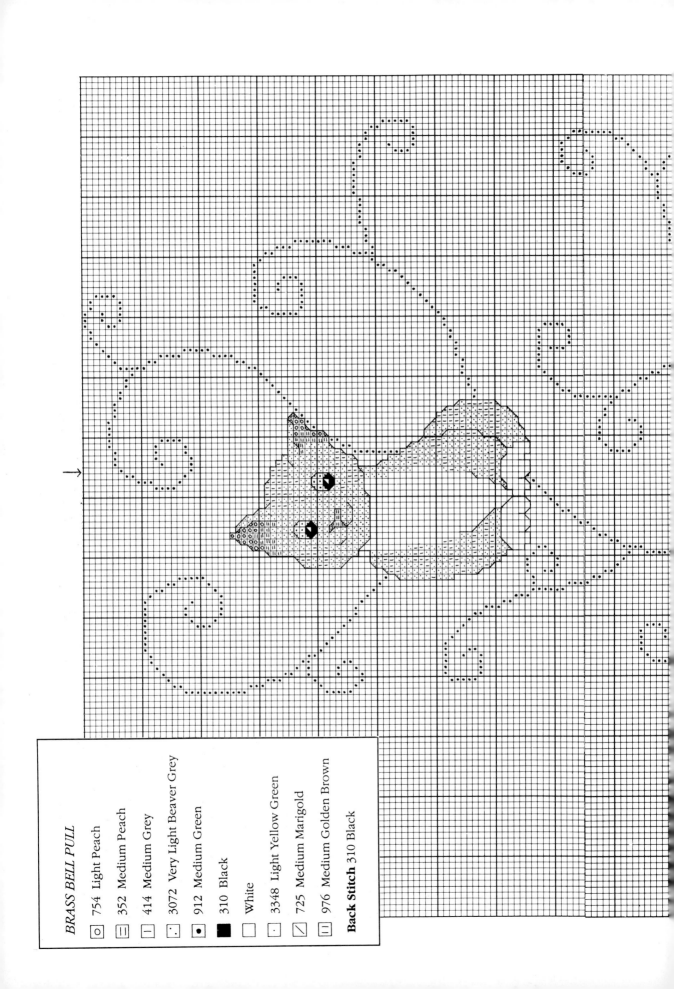

BRASS BELL PULL

○	754 Light Peach
=	352 Medium Peach
—	414 Medium Grey
∴	3072 Very Light Beaver Grey
●	912 Medium Green
■	310 Black
☐	White
·	3348 Light Yellow Green
╱	725 Medium Marigold
‖	976 Medium Golden Brown

Back Stitch 310 Black

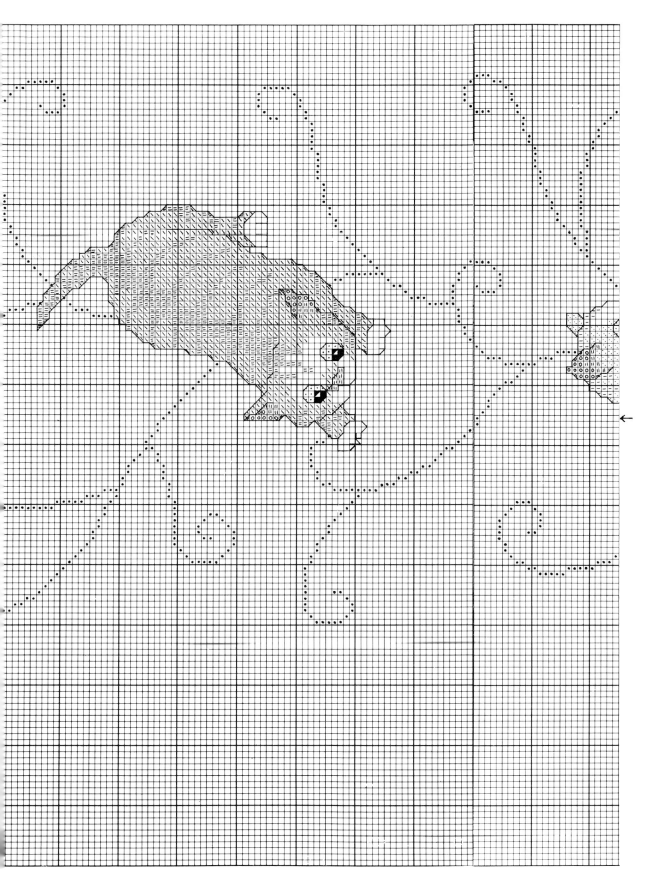

(chart continued on p54)

(chart continued from p53)

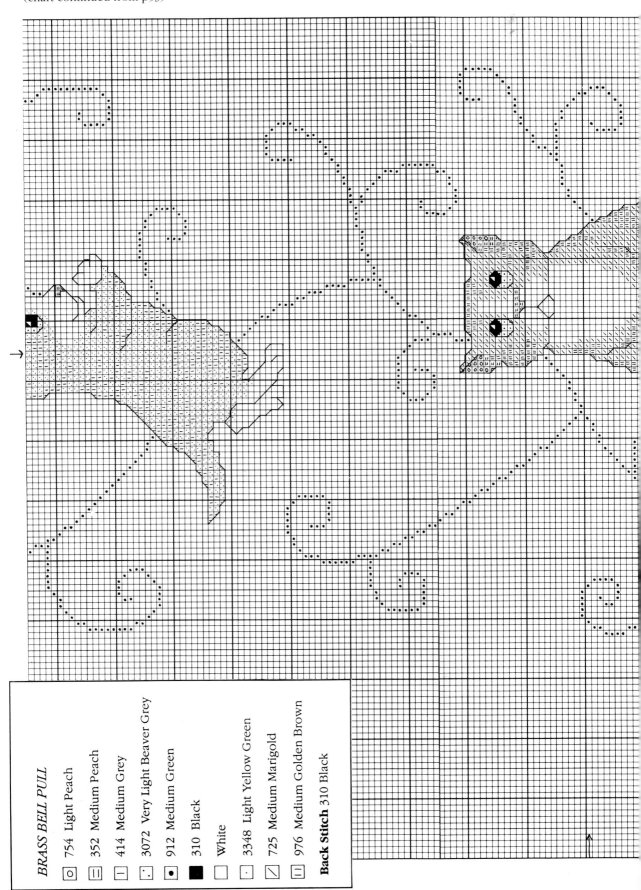

BRASS BELL PULL

○	754 Light Peach
=	352 Medium Peach
—	414 Medium Grey
∴	3072 Very Light Beaver Grey
●	912 Medium Green
■	310 Black
☐	White
·	3348 Light Yellow Green
╱	725 Medium Marigold
∐	976 Medium Golden Brown

Back Stitch 310 Black

(chart continued from p55)

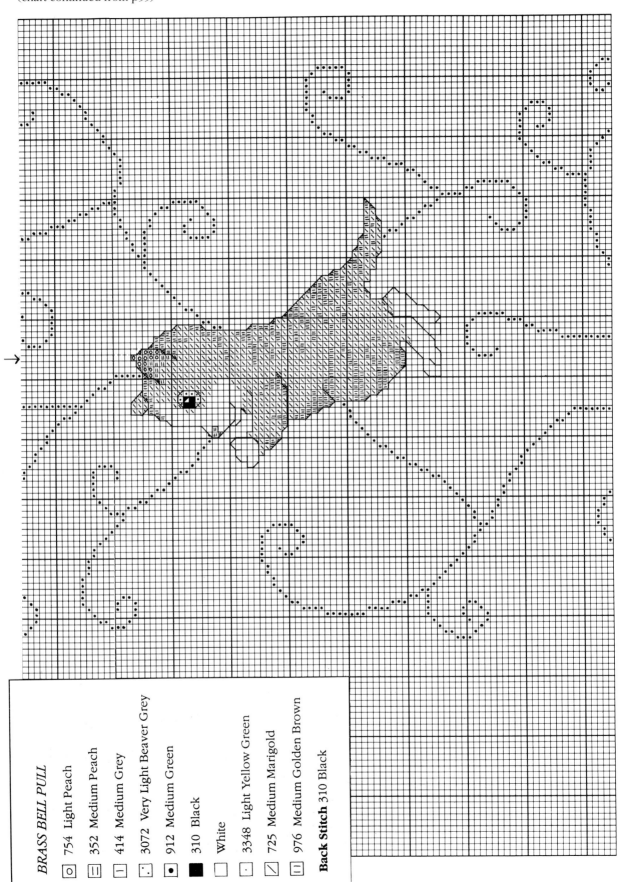

BRASS BELL PULL

⊡	754 Light Peach
⊟	352 Medium Peach
⊡	414 Medium Grey
⊡	3072 Very Light Beaver Grey
●	912 Medium Green
■	310 Black
☐	White
⊡	3348 Light Yellow Green
⧄	725 Medium Marigold
⊟	976 Medium Golden Brown

Back Stitch 310 Black

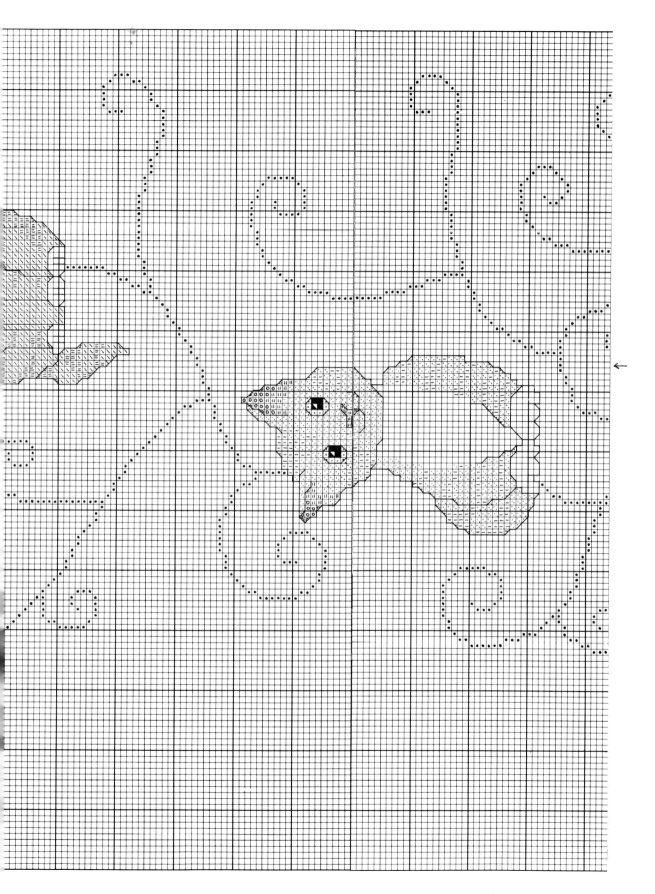

(chart continued on p56)

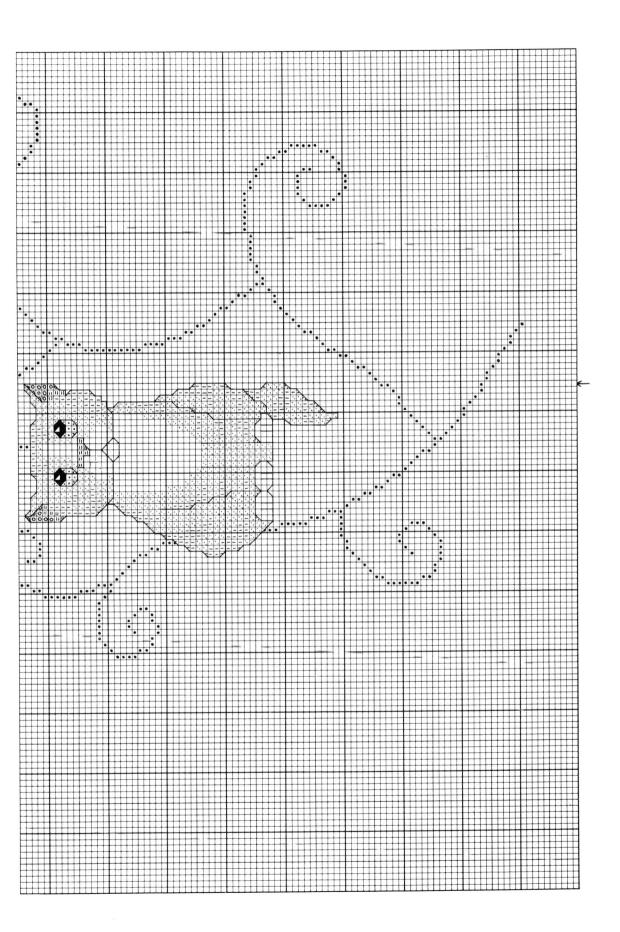

LACE-TRIMMED TABLE RUNNER

An enchanting row of cartoon cats examine the wonders of nature on a dainty table runner. It would fit happily anywhere in the home, but is especially suitable for a child's room, on a dressing table or chest of drawers. Although the chart is quite large, you will find it easy to follow.

MATERIALS

A piece of white Linda embroidery fabric with 27 threads to the inch (2.5cm), 24cm (9¹/₂in) deep x 80cm (31¹/₂in) wide
3.5m (4yd) white lace, 4cm (1¹/₂in) deep
DMC stranded cotton in the colours indicated
White sewing thread

(Finished size: 29 x 85cm /11 x 33in)

1 Work the design from the chart (pp 60-1), leaving slightly more clear fabric above the embroidery than below it. Use two strands of cotton for the cross-stitch and one strand for the backstitch.

(continued on p64)

(right) Mahogany-finish footstool and sewing box with cross-stitch (see p64)

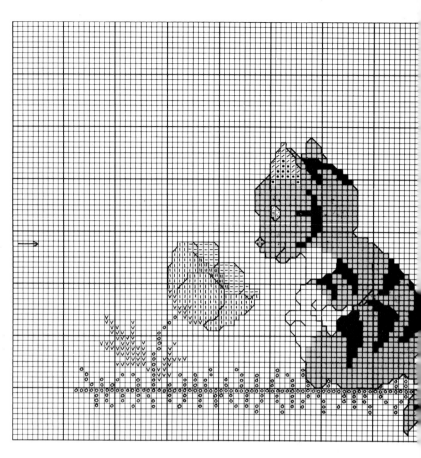

LACE-TRIMMED TABLE RUNNER

- ☐ 962 Rose Pink
- ☐ 963 Very Light Dusky Rose
- ☐ 727 Yellow
- ☐ 3347 Medium Avocado Green
- ☑ 3345 Dark Hunter Green
- ☐ White
- ■ 741 Medium Tangerine
- ▦ 744 Primrose Yellow
- ☐ 353 Peach
- ☐ 351 Coral
- ☐ 3348 Light Yellow Green
- ☐ 310 Black
- ☐ 898 Chocolate Brown

Back Stitch 310 Black

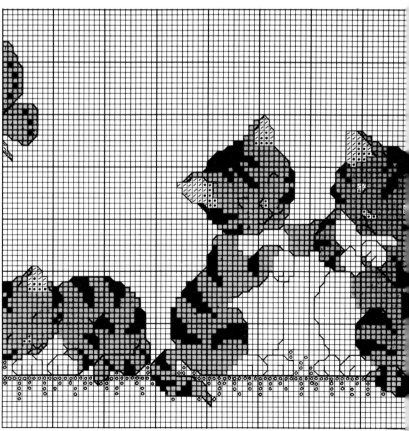

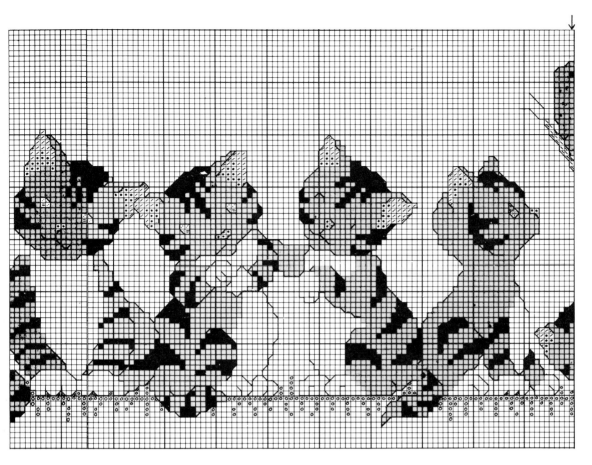
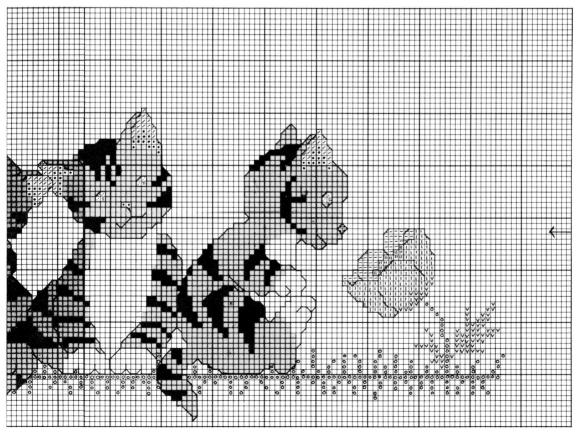

FOOTSTOOL

310	Black
646	Medium Grey
3024	Light Grey
725	Dark Gold
826	Medium Blue
824	Dark Blue
712	Off White
676	Tan
680	Dark Tan
841	Taupe
839	Brown
822	Light Beige (Table)
368	Light Pistachio Green
504	Light Grey/Green
472	Vy. Lt. Avocado Green
754	Flesh Pink
352	Rose Pink
350	Dark Rose Pink
828	Pale Sky Blue
Back Stitch	838 Dark Brown

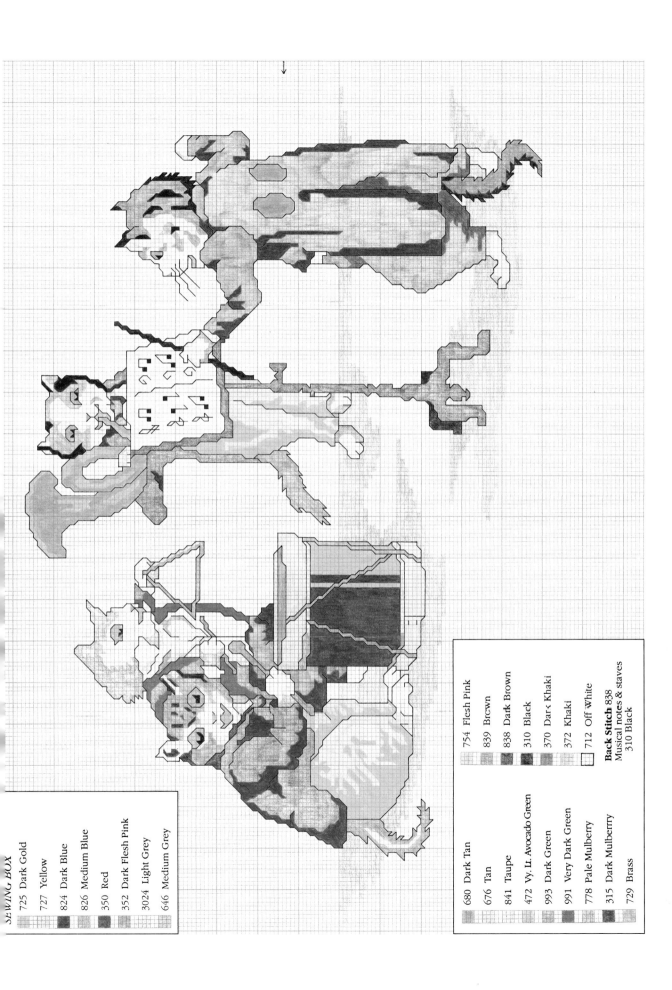

SEWING BOX

725 Dark Gold

727 Yellow

824 Dark Blue

826 Medium Blue

350 Red

352 Dark Flesh Pink

3024 Light Grey

646 Medium Grey

680 Dark Tan

676 Tan

841 Taupe

472 Vy. L. Avocado Green

993 Dark Green

991 Very Dark Green

778 Pale Mulberry

315 Dark Mulberry

729 Brass

754 Flesh Pink

839 Brown

838 Dark Brown

310 Black

370 Dark Khaki

372 Khaki

712 Off White

Back Stitch 838
Musical notes & staves
310 Black

2 Pin and tack a 1cm (³/8in) hem all round the edge of the fabric, mitring the corners (see Methods section).

3 Gather the straight edge of your lace, but don't draw it up. Mark the edge of the fabric, and the lace, into the same number of equal sections. Then pin the lace to the wrong side of the runner, matching the marked points and overlapping the edge as illustrated. Draw up the gathers to fit, distributing them evenly between the pins (allow a little extra at each corner).

4 Either machine or hand-stitch the lace into position.

FOOTSTOOL AND SEWING BOX

Two heirloom pieces with which to beautify your home (see p59). The amusing theme chosen for the embroidery upholstering the stool and sewing box features a lively set of cats in Victorian costume. Both pieces come to you as kits which you assemble yourself: the stool is made to accommodate a needlework design measuring 25 x 30cm (10 x 12in), and the sewing box takes a piece measuring 30 x 38cm (12 x 15in).

MATERIALS

A piece of cream Murano embroidery fabric with 30 threads to the inch (2.5cm), 40cm (15³/4in) deep x 45cm (17³/4in) wide, for the stool
A piece of cream Murano embroidery fabric with 30 threads to the inch (2.5cm), 45cm (17³/4in) deep x 53cm (20³/4in) wide, for the sewing box
Calico of the same size
DMC stranded cotton in the colours indicated

1 Work the embroidery designs (pp62–3) using two strands of DMC cotton for the cross-stitch, and one strand for the backstitch.

2 When the embroidery is finished, press the pieces carefully on the wrong side (see Methods section).

Then follow the manufacturer's instructions for mounting your work in the top of the stool and sewing box.

LACY BEDROOM SET

A striking collection of beautifully designed accessories to enhance your bedroom. The cottons used to embroider the cross-stitch designs are in variegated colours, which gives the work a particularly sophisticated elegance: whilst the delicate lace edging adds a final touch of nostalgic charm.

The complete set (pp66–7, 71) consists of two round cushions, two square cushions, lavender sachets and a nightdress bag. Each simple project features a different central design set against a slightly different background pattern.

NIGHTDRESS BAG

A fully lined bag in which to keep your nightie – so pretty that one forgets how very practical it is.

MATERIALS

Two pieces of ecru Ainring embroidery fabric with 18 stitches to the inch (2.5cm), approximately 47cm (18½in) deep x 42cm (16½in) wide
Two pieces of cream lining fabric, 46cm (18in) deep x 42cm (16½in) wide
2m (2yd) cream double-face satin ribbon, 2.5cm (1in) wide
DMC stranded cotton in the colours indicated
Sewing thread to match fabric
(Measurements include a 1cm/³⁄₈in seam allowance)

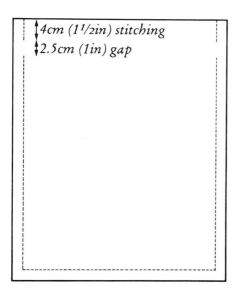

4cm (1½in) stitching
2.5cm (1in) gap

Fig 1

1 Work the cross-stitch design (p69)on one piece of Ainring for the front of the bag, using two strands of DMC cotton: position the embroidery so that you have 11.5cm (4½in) of clear fabric at each side, 10.5cm (4in) at the bottom, and 17cm (6⁵⁄₄in) at the top.

2 Place the two pieces of Ainring right sides together. Stitch the side seams down from the top for 4cm (1½in). Leave a gap of 3cm (1¼in), then recommence stitching the side seams to the bottom as figure 1.

(pp66-7) Lacy bedroom set: cushions and nightdress bag

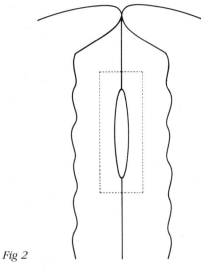

Fig 2

5 Turn to the right side and press, avoiding the embroidery if possible.
6 Place the two pieces of lining fabric right sides together and stitch the side seams. Then stitch the bottom seam, leaving 10cm (4in) open at the centre (figure 3). Clip the corners.
7 Place the outer bag into the lining, right sides together. Stitch around the top edge.
8 Turn right side out, easing through the opening at the bottom of the lining. Slip-stitch the lining together at the bottom.
9 Press the top edge of the bag along the seam.

3 Press the side seams open around the gap, and then top-stitch 5mm (¼in) from the edge, as figure 2.
4 Stitch the bottom seam and clip the corners.

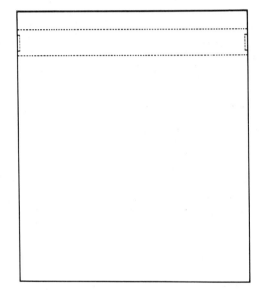

Fig 4

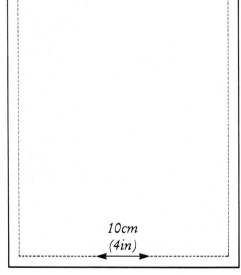

10cm
(4in)

Fig 3

10 Top-stitch around the bag 5mm (¼in) above the ribbon opening, and again below (figure 4).
11 Thread the ribbon twice through the channel formed by the two rows of stitches. Then join the ends and draw out a loop of ribbon at each side.

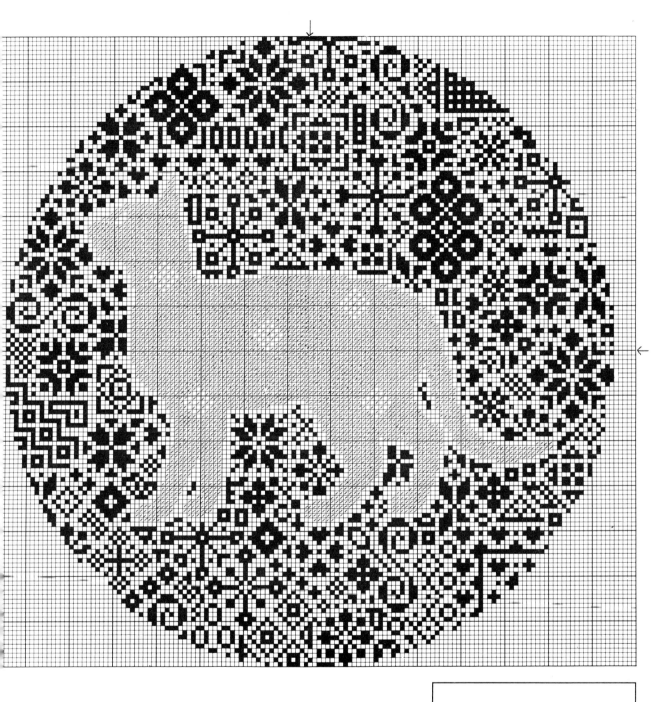

NIGHTDRESS BAG

■ 125 Varigated Green

▨ 954 Green

LAVENDER SACHETS

These dainty lace-trimmed lavender bags are far too pretty to be hidden away inside your wardrobe or chest of drawers. Hang them instead on the door or drawer knob, or on the bed-post, so that you can enjoy their fragrance to the full.

MATERIALS *(for each sachet)*
A 15cm (6in) square of cream or ecru Ainring embroidery fabric with 18 stitches to the inch (2.5cm)
A 15cm (6in) square of contrasting fabric to back
A small piece of muslin or thin fabric for the inner sachet
1m (1¼yd) off-white lace, 2.5cm (1in) deep
30cm (12in) cream or ecru double-face satin ribbon, 6mm (¼in) wide
Dried lavender
Small amount of kapok or polyester filling
DMC stranded cotton in the colours indicated
Sewing thread to match fabric
Fabric adhesive
(Measurements include a 1cm/³⁄₈in seam allowance)

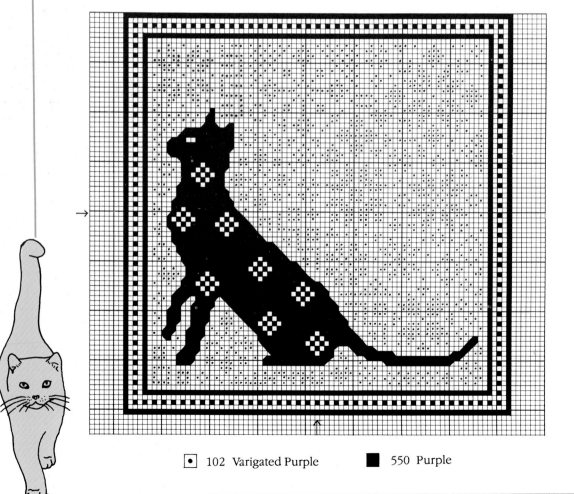

⊡ 102 Varigated Purple   ■ 550 Purple

1 Work the cross-stitch design centrally on the Ainring, using two strands of DMC cotton. When the embroidery is finished, press carefully on the wrong side (see Methods section).

2 Fold the ribbon in half and pin it to the right side of the sachet, the cut ends level with the top edge of the fabric, and the loop over the embroidered centre.

3 Gather the straight edge of the lace, but don't draw it up. Place your embroidery right side up on a flat surface, and pin the lace evenly round the sachet, right sides together, *with the outer edge of the lace towards the embroidered centre* and the straight edge extending just over the stitching line. Draw up the lace, distributing the gathers evenly between the pins (allow extra at the corners), and tack it into place. Stitch all round, along the seam line.

4 Place the backing fabric on top of the embroidered square, right sides together. Pin and then tack, taking care not to catch the lace in the seams.

5 Either machine or hand-stitch together, following the previous stitching line, and leaving an opening of about 4cm (1½in) on one side, for turning.

6 Remove the pins and tacking stitches, clip the corners and turn to the right side.

7 Make a lavender sachet from muslin or thin fabric and place it inside the bag, fixing it to the wrong side of the Ainring with a little fabric adhesive.

8 Stuff the bag lightly with kapok or alternative, pushing in small amounts at a time so that it is evenly filled.

9 Turn the raw edges of the opening inside and slip-stitch together.

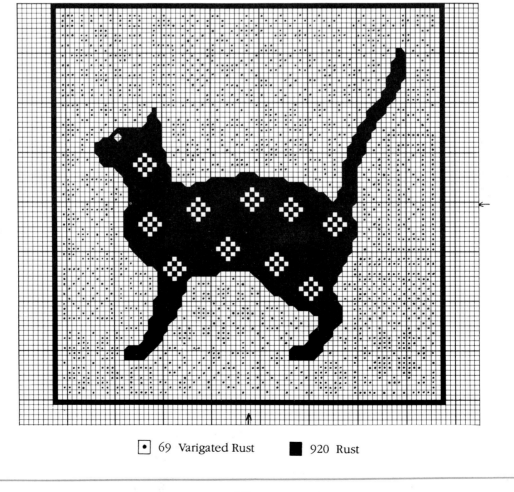

· 69 Varigated Rust   ■ 920 Rust

LACE-EDGED CUSHIONS

Frilled lace enhances the design on these lovely cushions (pp66–7) to scatter over the coverlet of a neatly made bed.

MATERIALS *(for each cushion)*

A 38cm (15in) square of cream or ecru Ainring embroidery fabric with 18 stitches to the inch (2.5cm), for the square cushion

A 38cm (15in) diameter circle of cream or ecru Ainring embroidery fabric with 18 stitches to the inch (2.5cm), for the round cushion

A piece of contrasting fabric of the same size, to back

3m (3½yd) cream or ecru lace, 5cm (2in) deep

A 36cm (14in) square cushion pad for the square cushion

A 36cm (14in) diameter circular cushion pad for the round cushion

DMC stranded cotton in the colours indicated

Sewing thread to match fabric

(Measurements include a 1cm/³⁄₈in seam allowance)

1 Work the chosen cross-stitch design (pp74–7) centrally on the Ainring, using two strands of DMC cotton. When the embroidery is finished, press carefully on the wrong side (see Methods section).

2 Gather the straight edge of the lace, but don't draw it up. Place your embroidery right side up on a flat surface, and pin the lace evenly round the cushion, right sides together, *with the outer edge of the lace towards the embroidered centre* and the straight edge extending just over the stitching line. Draw up the lace, distributing the gathers evenly between the pins, and tack it into place. Then stitch all round, along the seam line.

3 Place the backing fabric on top of the embroidered square or circle, right sides together. Pin and tack three sides of the square cushion, or three-quarters way round the outer edge of the circle, taking care not to catch the lace in the seams.

4 Machine-stitch the tacked seams, following the previous stitching line. Clip the corners, or trim and clip the curved edge. Then remove any pins and the tacking threads, and turn to the right side.

5 Press in the seam allowance along each side of the opening. Place the cushion pad inside the cover and oversew the edges together.

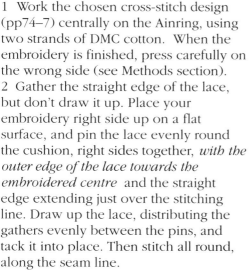

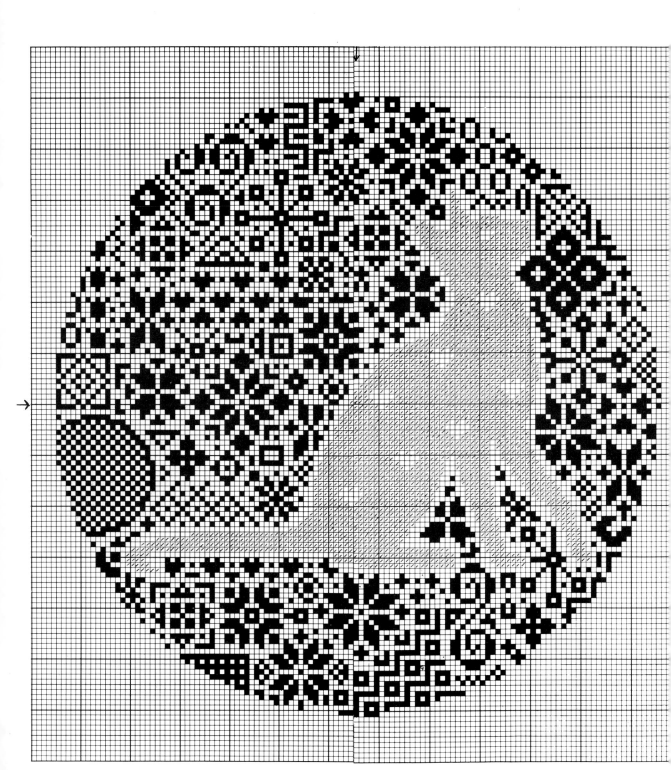

ROUND CUSHION (PINK)

■ 106 Varigated Pink

◪ 350 Pink

ROUND CUSHION (LILAC)

■ 52 Varigated Lilac

◪ 552 Lilac

SQUARE CUSHION (BLUE)

■ 103 Varigated Blue

⊿ 796 Royal Blue

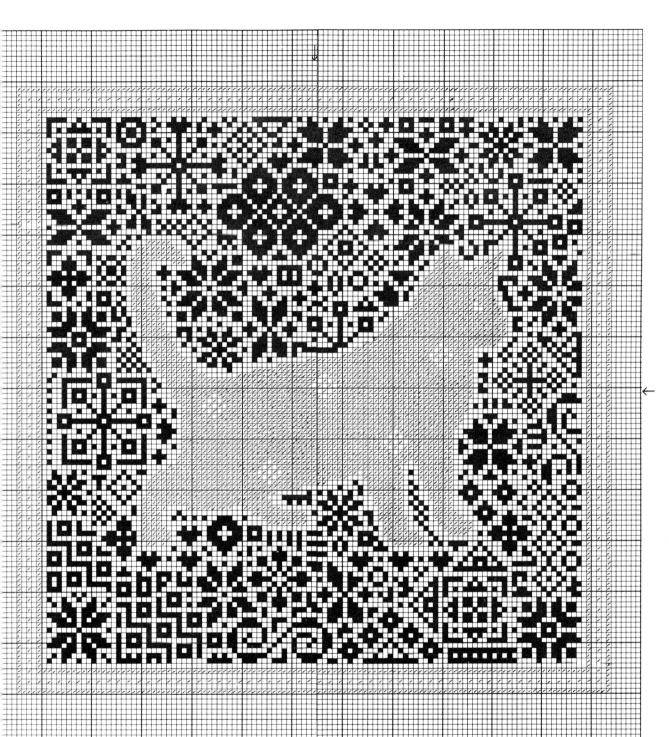

SQUARE CUSHION (DARK RED)

■ 75 Varigated Red

◿ 347 Dark Red

CHRISTMAS STOCKING

This very special stocking is just the right size to hold small toys and sweets to delight a child at Christmas. The decorative alphabet enables you to embroider the proud owner's name on the stocking, to make it even more personal.

MATERIALS

Two pieces of navy blue Ainring embroidery fabric with 18 stitches to the inch (2.5cm), approximately 24cm (9½in) deep x 17.5cm (7in) wide
1m (1yd) red bias binding
DMC stranded cotton in the colours indicated
Sewing thread to match the binding

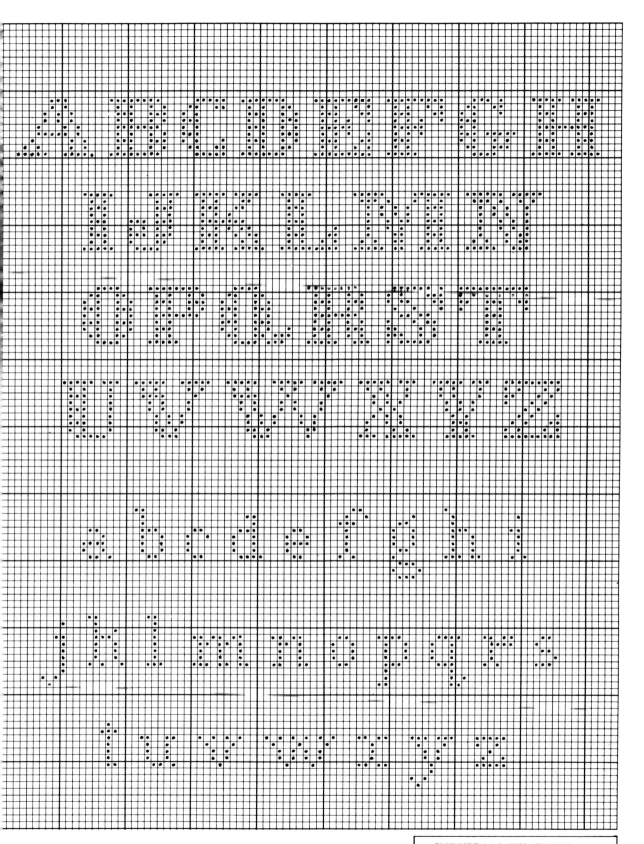

CHRISTMAS STOCKING

● 603 Bright Orange Red

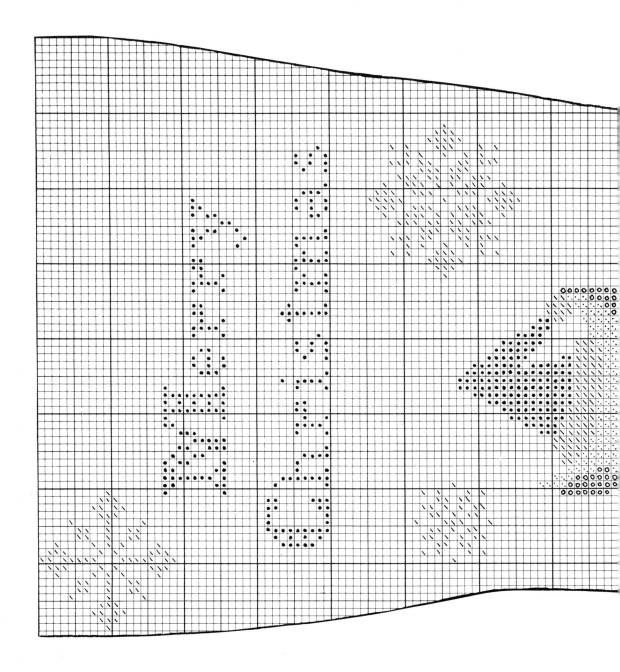

1 Work the cross-stitch design on one piece of fabric. Use two strands of DMC cotton for the cross-stitch, and one strand for the backstitch.

2 Using the chart as your pattern, cut two stocking shapes from the pieces of fabric.

3 Place the two pieces wrong sides together, and tack.

4 Machine-stitch around the stocking, leaving the top edge open. Trim the edge neatly 5mm (¼in) from the stitching line, and remove the tacking threads.

5 Bind the stitched edge, and all round the top edges, with bias binding. (See Kitchen Chair Pad: Section 1.)

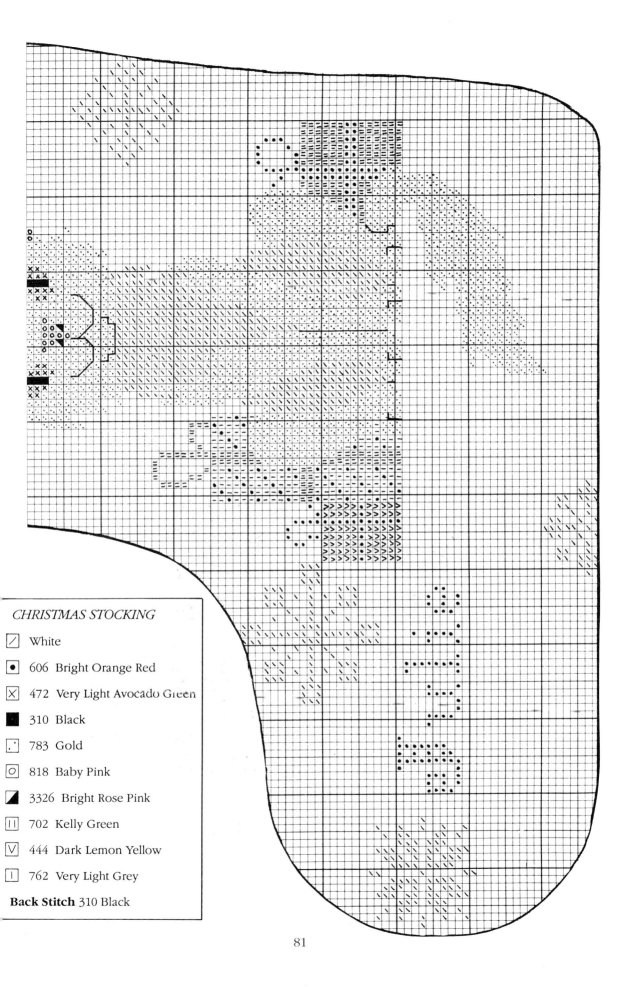

CHRISTMAS STOCKING

⟋		White
●	606	Bright Orange Red
✕	472	Very Light Avocado Green
■	310	Black
∴	783	Gold
○	818	Baby Pink
◣	3326	Bright Rose Pink
‖	702	Kelly Green
∨	444	Dark Lemon Yellow
❘	762	Very Light Grey

Back Stitch 310 Black

3
FRAMED CROSS-STITCH PICTURES

Walls were made for pictures! So what could be more appropriate than to display your handiwork – suitably framed – wherever it will be seen to advantage. Hang your pictures on your own walls for your own satisfaction, and for your friends to admire. Or give them as a special and delightful present.

Cat in the Window (Method: p83. Chart: p85)

MINIATURE: CAT WITH ROSE BORDER

CHART: p84   COLOUR PHOTOGRAPH: p86

An enchanting little picture that you will enjoy working. Why not embroider a set of three – all in different colourways – and group them together on your wall? Work the cross-stitch design from the chart, using two strands of embroidery coton.

MATERIALS
A 16cm (6¾in) square of pink Ainring embroidery fabric
with 18 stitches to the inch (2.5cm)
Press-On self-stick mounting board, 25 x 20cm (10 x 8in)
Alternatively, a piece of mounting board, approximately 13cm (5in) square
Masking tape
DMC stranded cotton in the colours indicated

PASTEL: UNDER THE RAINBOW

CHART: p84   COLOUR PHOTOGRAPH: p86

An unusual and most attractive design, that is extremely easy to do. Its very simplicity is its charm. Work the cross-stitch design from the chart, using two strands of embroidery cotton.

MATERIALS
A 24cm (9½in) square of sky blue Ainring embroidery
fabric with 18 stitches to the inch (2.5cm)
Press-On self-stick mounting board, 35 x 27.5cm (14 x 11in)
Alternatively, a piece of mounting board, approximately 21cm (8½in) square
Masking tape
DMC stranded cotton in the colours indicated

CAT IN THE WINDOW

CHART: p85   COLOUR PHOTOGRAPH: p82

A contented cat sits on the window-sill, deciding where to go tonight. What wicked plans are hidden behind that satisfied expression?! Work the design from the chart, using two strands of embroidery cotton for the cross-stitch, and one strand for the backstitch.

MATERIALS
A 27.5cm (11in) square of beige Linda embroidery fabric
with 27 threads to the inch (2.5cm)
Press-On self-stick mounting board, 35 x 27cm (14 x 11in)
Alternatively, a piece of mounting board, approximately 24.5cm (9½in) square
Masking tape
DMC stranded cotton in the colours indicated

MINIATURE: CAT WITH ROSE BORDER

· White

○ 351 Coral

╱ 818 Baby Pink

■ 702 Kelly Green

V 800 Pale Delft Blue

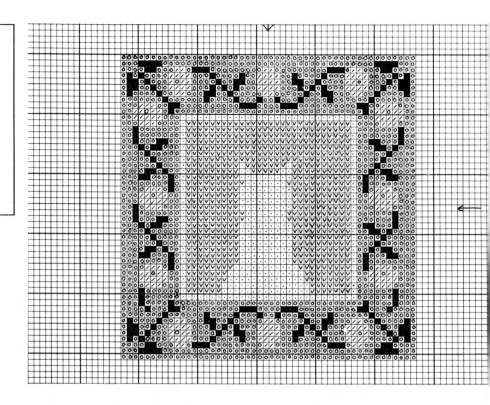

PASTEL: UNDER THE RAINBOW

● White

■ 321 Poppy Red

╱ 913 Medium Nile Green

I 963 Very Light Dusky Rose

○ 945 Flesh Pink

7 3078 Pale Yellow

C 772 Pale Citrus Green

X 809 Delft Blue

═ 775 Light Blue

V 210 Lilac

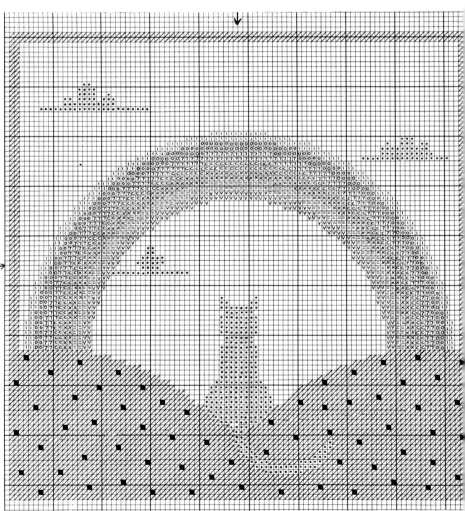

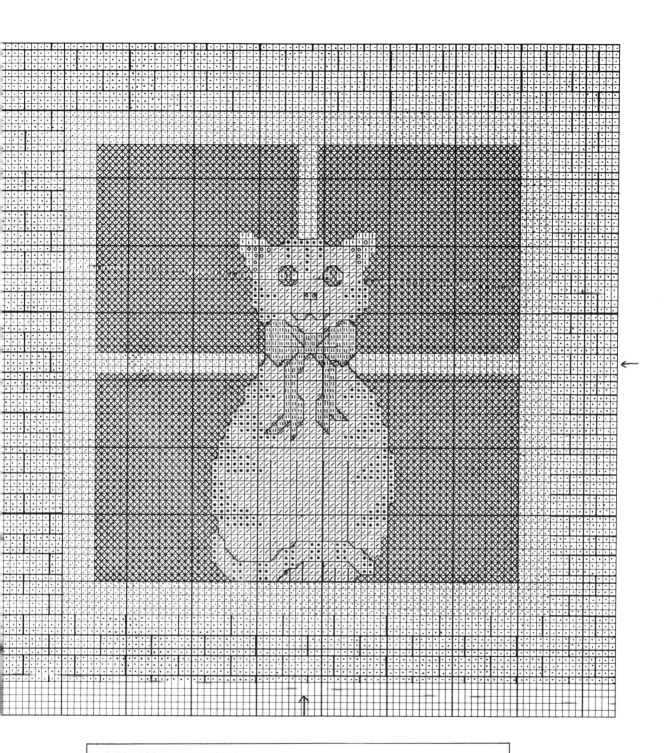

CAT IN THE WINDOW

Symbol	Code	Color
⊡	356	Melon Pink
⬚		White
⊠	310	Black
⊙	352	Medium Peach
⊥	754	Light Peach
⊘	725	Medium Marigold
⊙	976	Medium Golden Brown
‖	702	Kelly Green
⊟	3348	Light Yellow Green

Backstitch
Outline bricks 3033 Very Light
   Mocha Brown
Outline bow 699 Christmas Green

Miniature: Cat with Rose Border (Method: p83   Chart: p84)

Pastel: Under the Rainbow (Method: p83   Chart: p84)

SIAMESE KITTEN

CHART: p88 COLOUR PHOTOGRAPH: p90

A particularly attractive design that is a 'must' for every Siamese owner. In fact, could anyone fail to give in to that pleading expression?! Work the design from the chart, using two strands of embroidery cotton for the cross-stitch, and one strand for the backstitch.

MATERIALS

A piece of sage Ainring embroidery fabric with 18 stitches to the inch (2.5cm), 35.5cm (14in) deep x 30.5cm (12in) wide
Press-On self-stick mounting board, 50 x 40cm (20 x 16in)
Alternatively, a piece of mounting board, approximately 32.5 x 27.5cm (12¾ x 10¾in)
Masking tape
DMC stranded cotton in the colours indicated

TABBY KITTEN

CHART: p89 COLOUR PHOTOGRAPH: p91

He's not too sure about wearing that big bow – but it definitely makes him even more handsome! Work the design from the chart, using two strands of embroidery cotton for the cross-stitch, and one strand for the backstitch.

MATERIALS

A piece of ecru Ainring embroidery fabric with 18 stitches to the inch (2.5cm), 35.5cm (14in) deep x 31.5cm (12½in) wide
Press-On self-stick mounting board, 50 x 40cm (20 x 16in)
Alternatively, a piece of mounting board, approximately 32.5 x 28.5cm (12¾ x 11¼in)
Masking tape
DMC stranded cotton in the colours indicated

MODERN STYLE SAMPLER

CHART: pp92–4 COLOUR PHOTOGRAPH: p95

Samplers don't have to be old-fashioned. This amusing design, with its stylised cats, is quick and easy to work, and makes an eye-catching wall decoration. Work the cross-stitch design from the chart, using two strands of embroidery cotton.

MATERIALS

A piece of white Ainring embroidery fabric with 18 stitches to the inch (2.5cm), 44.5cm (17½in) deep x 30.5cm (12in) wide
Press-On self-stick mounting board, 50 x 40cm (20 x 16in)
Alternatively, a piece of mounting board, approximately
41.5 x 27.5cm (16¼ x 10¾in)
Masking tape
DMC stranded cotton in the colours indicated

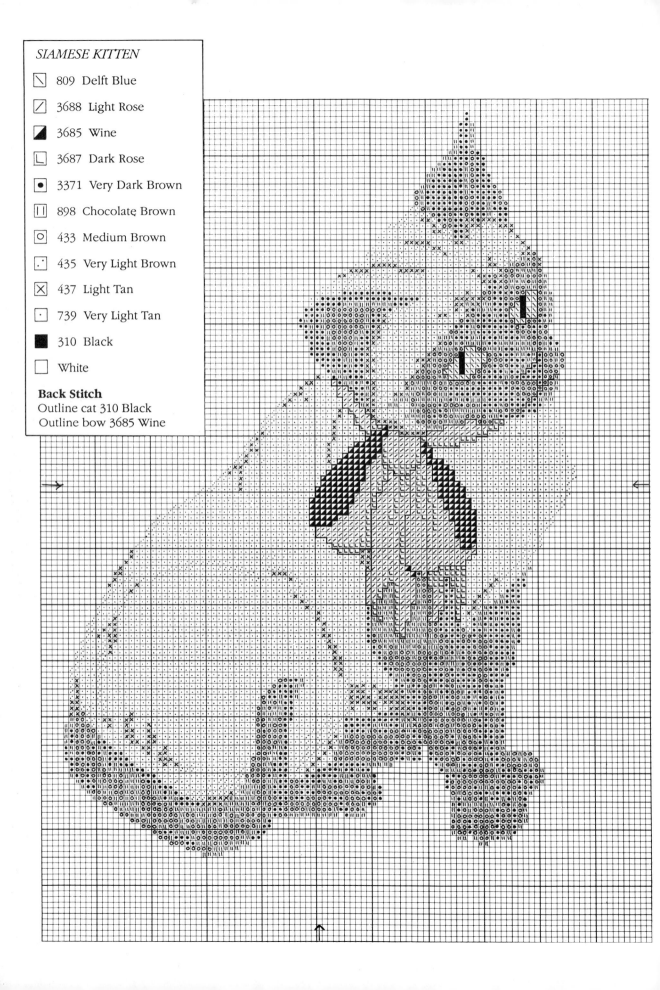

SIAMESE KITTEN

⊡	809	Delft Blue
⊘	3688	Light Rose
◪	3685	Wine
∟	3687	Dark Rose
⊙	3371	Very Dark Brown
‖	898	Chocolate Brown
○	433	Medium Brown
⸱	435	Very Light Brown
✕	437	Light Tan
·	739	Very Light Tan
■	310	Black
☐		White

Back Stitch
Outline cat 310 Black
Outline bow 3685 Wine

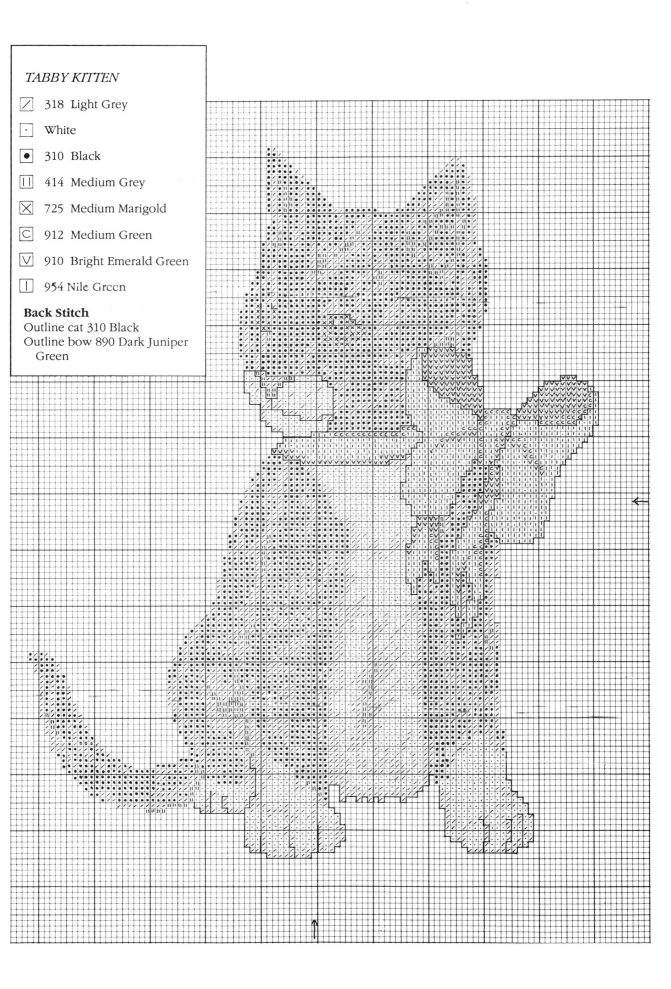

TABBY KITTEN

Symbol	Code	Colour
╱	318	Light Grey
·		White
●	310	Black
‖	414	Medium Grey
✕	725	Medium Marigold
C	912	Medium Green
V	910	Bright Emerald Green
I	954	Nile Green

Back Stitch
Outline cat 310 Black
Outline bow 890 Dark Juniper
Green

Siamese Kitten (Method: p87   Chart: p88)

Tabby Kitten (Method: p87   Chart: p89)

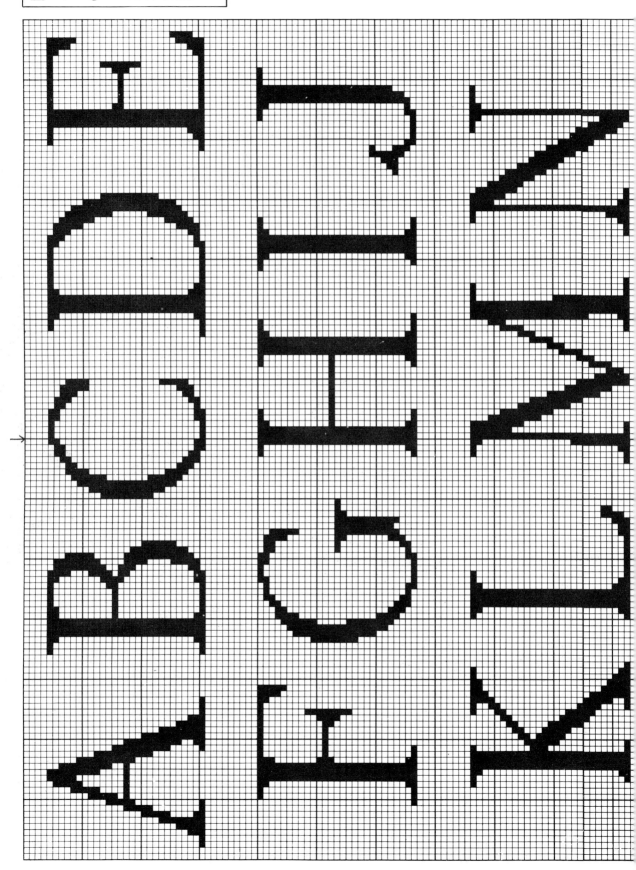

(chart continued from p93)

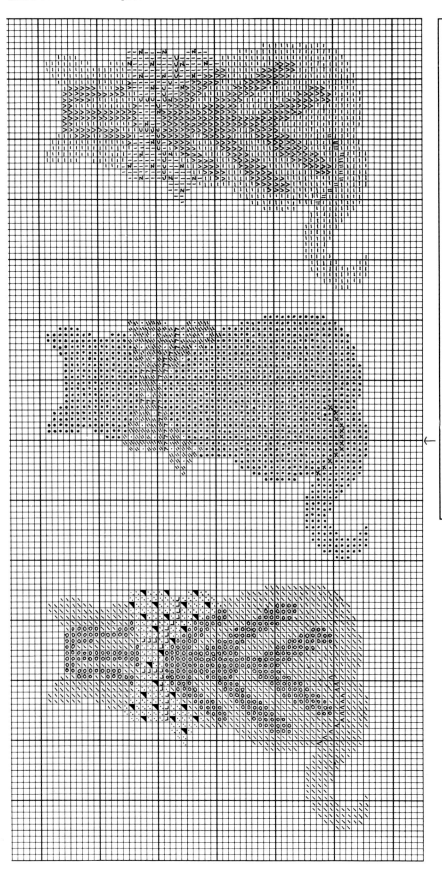

(chart continued on p94)

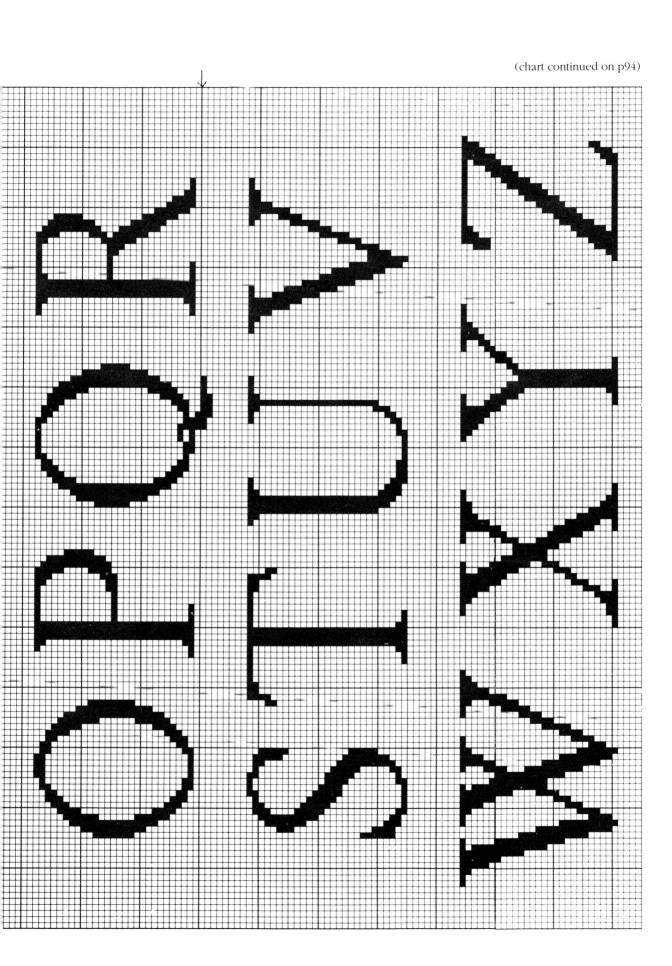

Modern Style Sampler (Method: p87 Chart pp92 – 4)

BLACK AND WHITE KITTEN

CHART: p97   COLOUR PHOTOGRAPH: p98

There's something specially appealing about a tiny black and white kitten... Who could possibly resist this one?! Work the design from the chart, using two strands of embroidery cotton for the cross-stitch, and one strand for the backstitch.

MATERIALS

A 33cm (13in) square of pink Ainring embroidery fabric with 18 stitches to the inch
(2.5cm)
Press-On self-stick mounting board, 50 x 40cm (20 x 16in)
Alternatively, a piece of mounting board, approximately 30cm (12in) square
Masking tape
DMC stranded cotton in the colours indicated

FLORAL CAT WITH BUTTERFLY

CHART: p100   COLOUR PHOTOGRAPH: p99

A charming design reminiscent of those elegant flower-painted china cats that look so graceful sitting beside the fireplace or on a mantelpiece. The butterfly adds a delightful finishing touch. Work the design from the chart, using two strands of embroidery cotton for the cross-stitch, and one strand for the backstitch.

MATERIALS

A piece of grey Ainring embroidery fabric with 18 stitches to the inch (2.5cm), 29cm
(11½in) deep x 25.5cm (10in) wide
Press-On self-stick mounting board, 35 x 27.5cm (14 x 11in)
Alternatively, a piece of mounting board, approximately 26 x 22.5cm (10¼ x 9in)
Masking tape
DMC stranded cotton in the colours indicated

ANTIQUE STYLE CAT SAMPLER

CHART: p101   COLOUR PHOTOGRAPH: p99

The perfect sampler for any cat lover! The well-fed tabby, flanked by pots of flowers, has all the nostalgic charm of early nineteenth-century needlework. Work the design from the chart, using two strands of embroidery cotton for the cross-stitch, and one strand for the backstitch.

MATERIALS

A piece of beige Linda embroidery fabric with 27 threads to the inch (2.5cm), 18cm (7in)
deep x 33cm (13in) wide
Press-On self-stick mounting board, 27.5 x 35cm (11 x 14in)
Alternatively, a piece of mounting board, approximately 15 x 30cm (6 x 12in)
Masking tape
DMC stranded cotton in the colours indicated

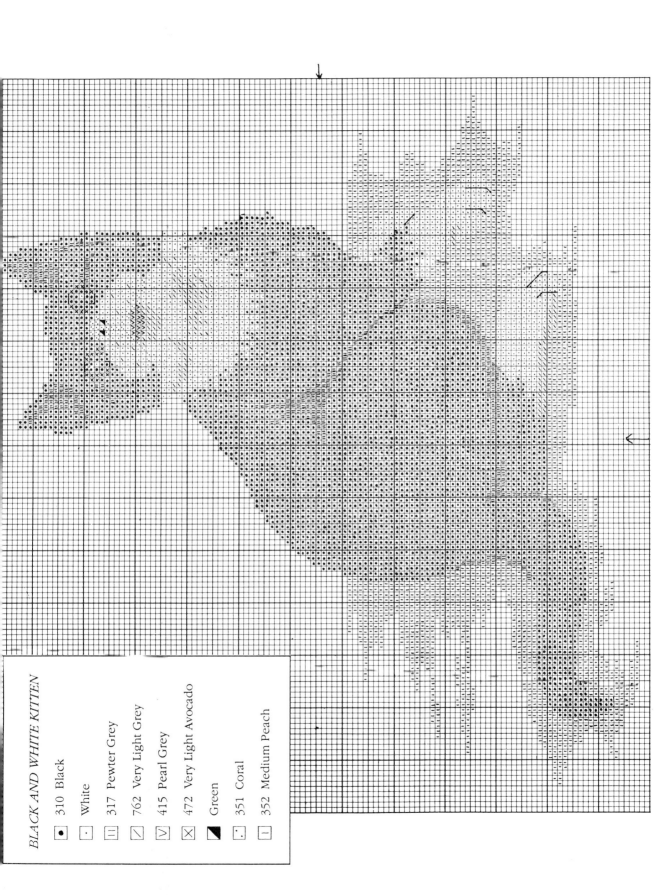

BLACK AND WHITE KITTEN

●	310 Black
·	White
‖	317 Pewter Grey
╱	762 Very Light Grey
⋁	415 Pearl Grey
☒	472 Very Light Avocado
◢	Green
⸪	351 Coral
▯	352 Medium Peach

Black and White Kitten (Method: p96   Chart: p97)

Floral Cat with Butterfly (Method: p96   Chart: p100)

Antique Style Cat Sampler (Method: p96   Chart: p101)

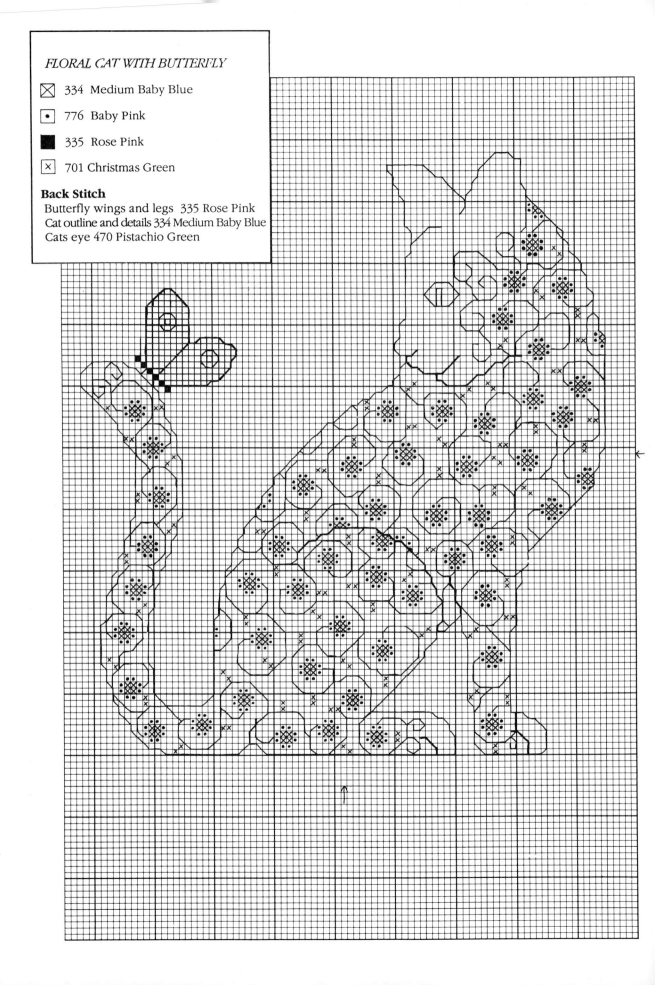

FLORAL CAT WITH BUTTERFLY

⊠ 334 Medium Baby Blue

• 776 Baby Pink

■ 335 Rose Pink

☒ 701 Christmas Green

Back Stitch
Butterfly wings and legs 335 Rose Pink
Cat outline and details 334 Medium Baby Blue
Cats eye 470 Pistachio Green

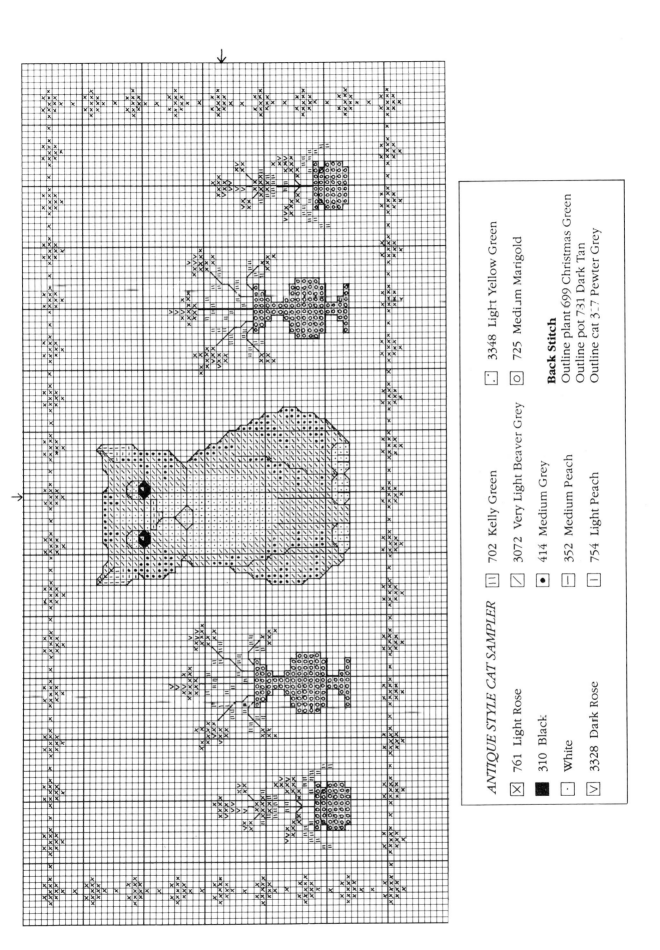

ANTIQUE STYLE CAT SAMPLER

X	761 Light Rose
■	310 Black
·	White
V	3328 Dark Rose

‖	702 Kelly Green
/	3072 Very Light Beaver Grey
•	414 Medium Grey
–	352 Medium Peach
I	754 Light Peach

∴	3348 Light Yellow Green
○	725 Medium Marigold

Back Stitch

Outline plant 699 Christmas Green
Outline pot 731 Dark Tan
Outline cat 317 Pewter Grey

ORGAN GRINDER

A most attractive design with a definite period flavour. The storybook subject is fun to embroider, and the finished picture will make a colourful wall decoration wherever it is hung. Work the design from the chart, using two strands of embroidery cotton for the cross-stitch, and one strand for the backstitch.

MATERIALS
A piece of cream Linda embroidery fabric with 27 threads to the inch (2.5cm), 37cm (15in) deep x 35cm (14in) wide
Press-On self-stick mounting board, 50 x 40cm (20 x 16in)
Alternatively, a piece of mounting board, approximately 34 x 32cm (13½ x 12½in)
Masking tape
DMC stranded cotton in the colours indicated

725 Dark Gold	472 Vy. Lt. Avocado Green	646 Medium Grey	824 Dark Blue
727 Yellow	350 Dark Rose Pink	3024 Light Grey	828 Pale Sky Blue
310 Black	352 Rose Pink	841 Taupe	503 Grey Green
754 Flesh Pink	436 Tan	839 Brown	504 Pale Grey Green
948 Light Flesh Pink	738 Light Tan	826 Medium Blue	712 Off White

Back Stitch 838 Dark Brown

MOUNTING CROSS-STITCH EMBROIDERIES

First, cut your mounting board to the required size for your finished picture, making sure that you will have 2.5–4cm (1–1½in) surplus embroidery fabric extending all round the board: trim the fabric to this size (making it altogether 5–8cm/2–3in wider and deeper than the board).

Before mounting your cross-stitch picture, press the completed embroidery carefully, right side down, on a softly padded surface, under a damp cloth. Then wait until it is dry, keeping it quite flat.

To stretch your embroidery over the mounting board, place it face down on a clean flat surface (if possible, don't move it after pressing), and position the board centrally on top. Rest a heavy book or similar weight in the centre, to prevent the board moving: you may also find it helpful to use a dry stick adhesive (UHU Stic), or Double Stick Scotch tape, on the right side of the board before placing it on the back of the embroidery, as this will ensure there is no movement.

Mitre each corner very carefully, cutting the fabric just a fraction away from the corner of the board. (Mitred corners: see Methods section at the beginning of the book.)

Fold one edge of the fabric over the mounting board (check to make sure that the threadline of the fabric is absolutely straight), and secure it with pins along the edge of the board. Fix the opposite edge in the same way, again checking that the fabric is straight and taut on the

board. Use masking tape to secure the edges of the fabric smoothly to the back of the mounting board, and then remove the pins. Repeat this procedure for the remaining two edges.

Alternatively, there is a specially prepared board available (made by Press-On Products Inc.) that simplifies the job considerably, whilst ensuring accurate positioning and correctly aligned edges. These self-stick mounting boards are available in a range of five sizes, from most large stores and good craft shops.

Prepare your embroidery and cut the Press-On mounting board to size as before. Then peel the backing off the board and place it centrally over the back of the needlework, with the edges straight to the threadline of the fabric. When you are quite satisfied, press down very hard over the entire surface. If necessary, turn the whole thing over very carefully and press the fabric down onto the board to ensure it is firmly stuck.

With the right side down again, mitre the corners (as above). Then fold the excess fabric neatly over each side and tape it to the back of the board.

Your embroidered picture is now ready to be framed. Unless you have experience in this craft, you will find it more satisfactory to take your work to a professional framer. If you are having glass in the frame, you will probably find that the non-reflective type is worth the additional expense.

4

NEEDLEPOINT
PROJECTS

BASIC NEEDLEPOINT TECHNIQUES

Needlepoint is worked with wool or thread over canvas, and the stitches cover the whole area, including the background. This means that the finished embroidery is strong and heavy, and very durable, making it particularly suitable for upholstery and soft furnishings, such as footstools, cushion covers, chair seats, rugs and decorative wall hangings. It is also ideal for small, practical items like spectacles cases and purses.

CANVAS

There are two types of canvas in general use: one is woven with single threads, and the other with double threads. The size of mesh varies, giving more or less stitches to the inch (2.5cm), so it is important that the wool or thread used for the embroidery is carefully matched to the canvas, to ensure complete coverage, whilst allowing it to pass easily through the holes in the canvas.

All the following needlepoint designs are worked on ten stitches to the inch (2.5cm) double-mesh canvas, using DMC tapestry wool. This is a superior quality non-divisible 4-ply wool which is mothproof and colourfast. It comes in a fully comprehensive range of colours and shades, enabling you to achieve subtle blendings and shaded effects.

WORKING THE NEEDLEPOINT

The designs are shown in chart form: each square on the chart represents one needlepoint stitch to be taken on the canvas, and each different symbol represents a colour. All the designs are worked in tent stitch (or half cross-stitch), using DMC tapestry wool.

It is advisable to work needlepoint on a rotating wooden frame: either a floor-standing model for larger projects, or a hand-held frame for smaller ones. Both are available in several sizes. The frame holds the canvas at a permanent tension: this makes it easier to work, keeps the stitching even, and helps to maintain the shape of the canvas until the needlepoint is finished. Don't use a hoop, as they are unsuitable for canvas work.

If you decide to work without a frame, you may find that the raw edges of the canvas damage the wool as you sew, and also snag your clothing. To avoid this happening, bind the rough edges with masking tape.

If the yarn becomes twisted whilst working, hold the needlepoint up and let the needle and yarn hang down to allow it to untwist. Don't continue working with twisted yarn, as it will appear thinner and will not cover the canvas properly.

(pp 106–7) Rectangular cushion covers Harold (*right*) and Marmaduke (*left*), with square cushion Wibur

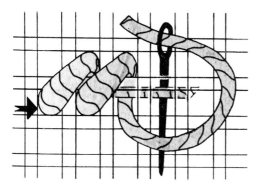

Fig 1

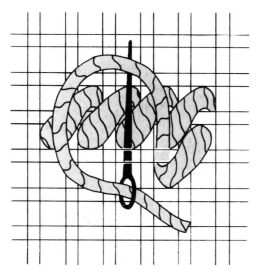

Fig 2

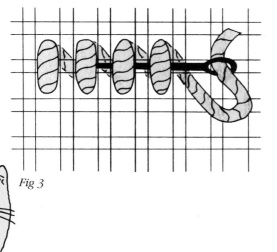

Fig 3

STITCHING TECHNIQUES

Always work the tent stitches so that they slant from left to right. Start at the top left-hand corner of the design: bring the needle from the back to the front of the canvas (see arrow on figure 1), leaving about 2–3cm (1in) of yarn at the back. This will be sewn in when the first few stitches are made (do *not* make knots to secure the yarn). Now take the needle diagonally up to the right, pushing it down through the next hole in the row above: then bring it back through the hole immediately below as shown in figure 1. Work the rows straight from left to right, so that the stitches are vertical on the wrong side of the canvas (as in figure 3).

When working small areas of a design, stitch to the end of each row: then turn the canvas upside down to work the next row. Alternatively, simply stitch from right to left, without turning the canvas, as figure 2. The end of the finished thread should be worked in on the wrong side of the work, as figure 3.

It is necessary to leave a border around the finished needlepoint design, to allow for stretching and making up. The border allowance and full directions are given with each project.

STRETCHING NEEDLEPOINT

If you haven't worked your embroidery on a frame, you will probably find that the finished needlepoint has pulled slightly out of shape: in which case it will require stretching before it can be made up. If you are having the embroidery framed, this will be done for you.

However, it is easy to do oneself. You will need a firm board, slightly larger than your canvas; some rust-proof tacks; a sheet of blotting paper; and a sheet of graph paper slightly larger than your needlepoint design. (See diagram.)

1 Cover the board with graph paper, then draw the outline shape on the paper, about 5cm (2in) larger than your piece of needlepoint.

2 Cut the blotting paper to the same size as the worked section of needlepoint, then place it on top of the graph paper to absorb the moisture when the needlepoint is dampened.

3 Pin out the needlepoint, face downwards on top of the botting paper, using the rust-proof tacks. Pull the canvas gently into shape, using the squares on the graph paper to check that it is correctly aligned. Pin all four edges, placing the tacks 5mm (¼in) apart.

4 Using a damp cloth, gently dampen the needlepoint with water, taking great care not to make it too wet: on no account *soak* the canvas. Then leave it to dry. Dampening the needlepoint in this way softens the gum which is used to stiffen the canvas threads, and they will re-set in the correct position as they dry.

5 After twenty-one days, the tacks may be carefully removed. If the needlepoint has been pulled badly out of shape, the stretching process may need to be repeated.

Stretching needlepoint

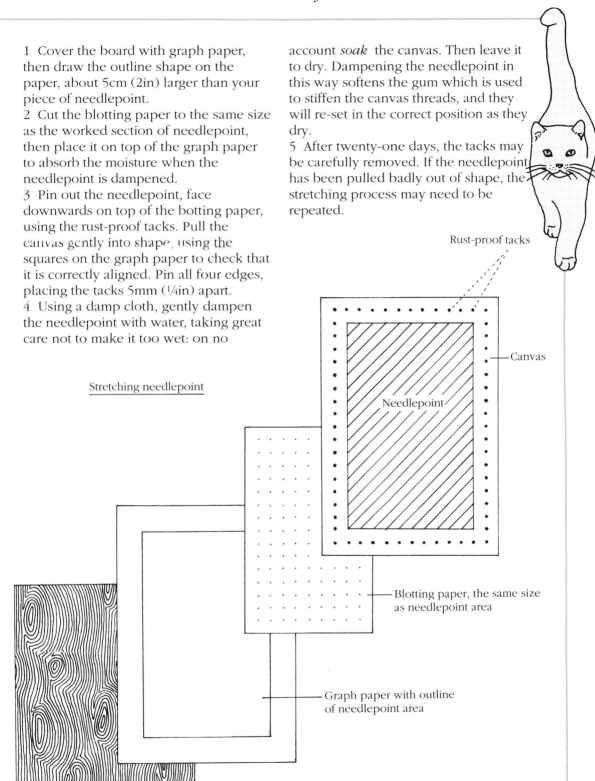

Rust-proof tacks

Canvas

Needlepoint

Blotting paper, the same size as needlepoint area

Graph paper with outline of needlepoint area

Board

CUSHION COVERS

A striking set of cushions that will make an eye-catching feature in any room. When choosing your backing fabric, bear in mind that you will need something of a similar weight to the finished needlepoint. Velvet, Dralon and other medium-to-heavyweight curtain fabrics are ideal.

'HAROLD', 'MARMADUKE' AND 'CARTOON CAT'

MATERIALS for each rectangular cushion
Finished size: 35.5 x 48cm/14 x 19in
A piece of double-thread canvas with 10 stitches to the inch (2.5cm), 48.5cm (19in) deep x 61cm (24in) wide
A piece of contrasting backing fabric, 40.5cm (16in) deep x 53.5cm (21in) wide
50cm (⅝yd) calico, 90cm (36in) wide
OR 40cm (½yd) calico, 115cm (45in) wide
Kapok or washable polyester filling
DMC tapestry wool in the colours indicated
Matching sewing thread

'APPLIQUÉ STYLE CATS' AND 'WILBUR'

MATERIALS for each square cushion
Finished size: 35.5cm/14in square
A 48.5cm (19in) square of double-thread canvas with 10 stitches to the inch (2.5cm)
A 40.5cm (16in) square of contrasting backing fabric
A 36cm (14in) square cushion pad
DMC tapestry wool in the colours indicated
Matching sewing thread

Rectangular Cushion Pad

1 Cut two 35.5 x 48.5cm (14 x 19in) rectangles of calico.
2 Pin the pieces together, right sides inside, and join all round, leaving an opening of about 10cm (4in) at one side. Clip the corners and turn to right side.
3 Stuff firmly, then turn in the raw edges of the opening and slip-stitch together.

Making up the Cushions

1 When you have completed your embroidery, trim the canvas, leaving a 2.5cm (1in) border of unworked canvas all round the needlepoint.
2 Place the needlepoint and the backing fabric together with right sides facing: machine-stitch around three sides of a square cushion, or two long sides and one short one of a rectangle, stitching as close as possible to the worked area.
3 Mitre the canvas at each corner, then press the seams open and turn the cushion to the right side.
4 Insert the cushion pad, then turn in the canvas and backing at the open end and slip-stitch neatly together, level with the edge of the needlepoint.

(*right*) Appliqué Style Cats (square cusion) with Cartoon Cat cushion and (*left*) the pin cusion (see p43).

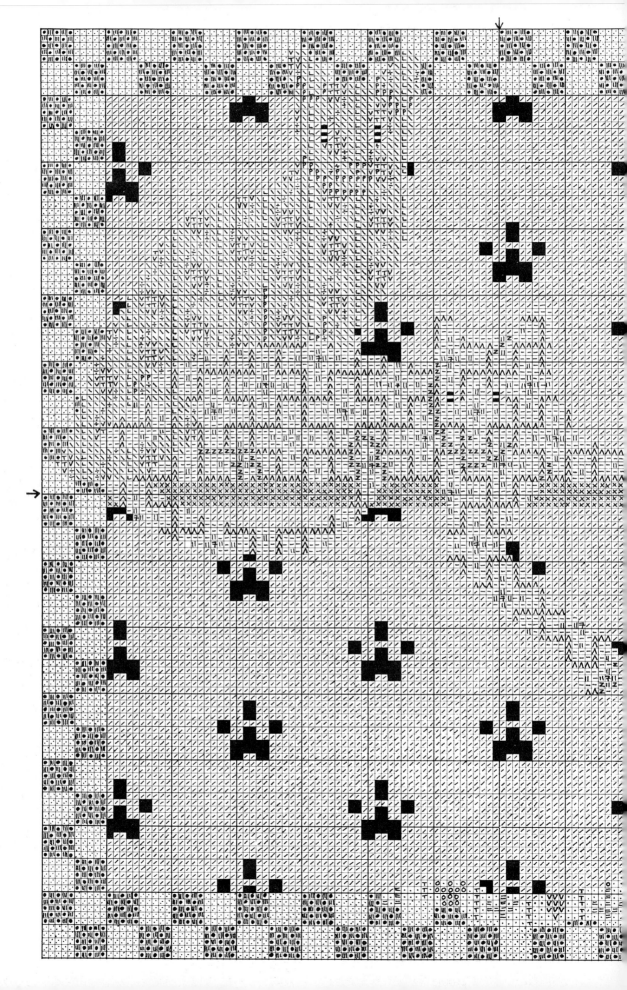

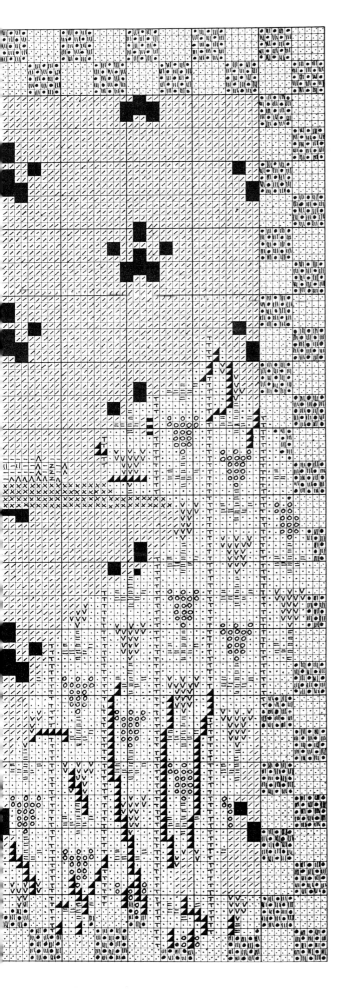

APPLIQUÉ STYLE CATS

⊡	7198	Maroon
⫴	7347	Dark Green
⦂	7344	Medium Green
■	7146	Dark Flesh Pink
⁄	7591	Dark Air Force Blue
◢	7463	Beige
⊤	7241	Lilac
⊠	7508	Tan
Ⴭ	7195	Dark Pink
P	7748	Dark Yellow
⌊	7800	Pale Blue
▬	7740	Orange
∨	7102	Baby Pink
○	7247	Mauve
⊒	7769	Pistachio Green
·	7451	Ecru
∧	7542	Pastel Green
‖	7798	Blue
⨕	7708	Light Mauve
−	7211	Pale Pink
÷	7770	Light Pistachio Green
╲	7078	Pale Yellow

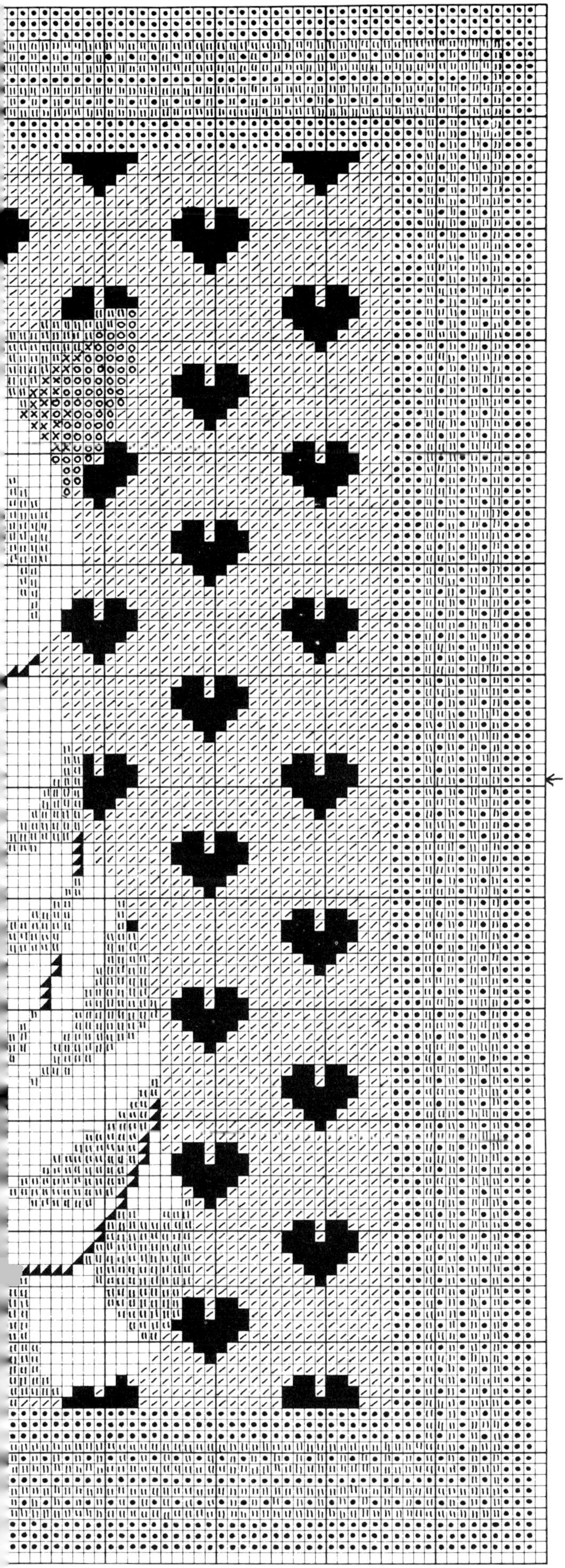

WILBUR

- Black
- 7620 Pewter Grey
- 7245 Mauve
- 7727 Yellow
- 7121 Flesh Pink
- 7124 Dark Flesh Pink
- 7715 Pale Grey
- 7400 Off White
- White
- 7624 Graphite Grey
- 7918 Amber

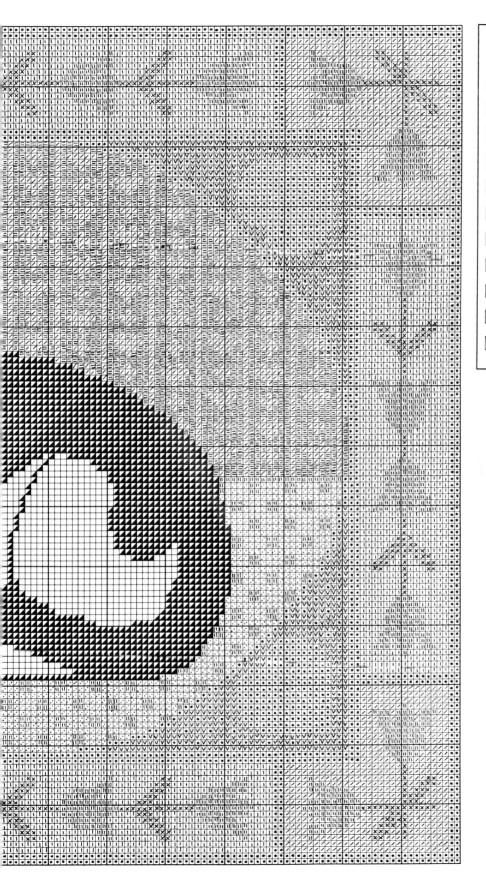

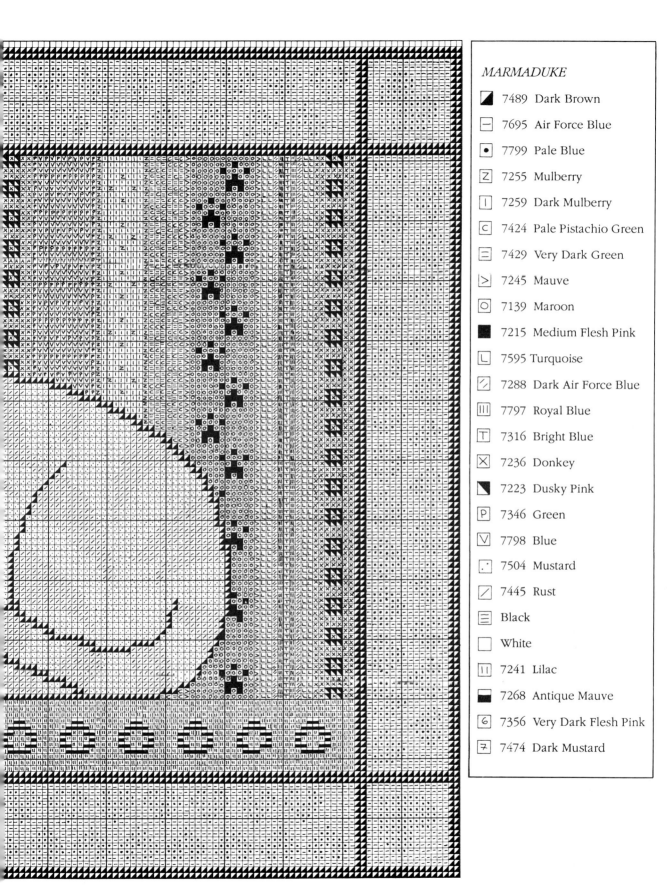

MARMADUKE

Symbol	Code	Colour
◢	7489	Dark Brown
−	7695	Air Force Blue
•	7799	Pale Blue
Z	7255	Mulberry
I	7259	Dark Mulberry
C	7424	Pale Pistachio Green
=	7429	Very Dark Green
>	7245	Mauve
O	7139	Maroon
■	7215	Medium Flesh Pink
L	7595	Turquoise
/	7288	Dark Air Force Blue
III	7797	Royal Blue
T	7316	Bright Blue
X	7236	Donkey
◣	7223	Dusky Pink
P	7346	Green
V	7798	Blue
∴	7504	Mustard
/	7445	Rust
≡		Black
☐		White
II	7241	Lilac
▬	7268	Antique Mauve
6	7356	Very Dark Flesh Pink
7	7474	Dark Mustard

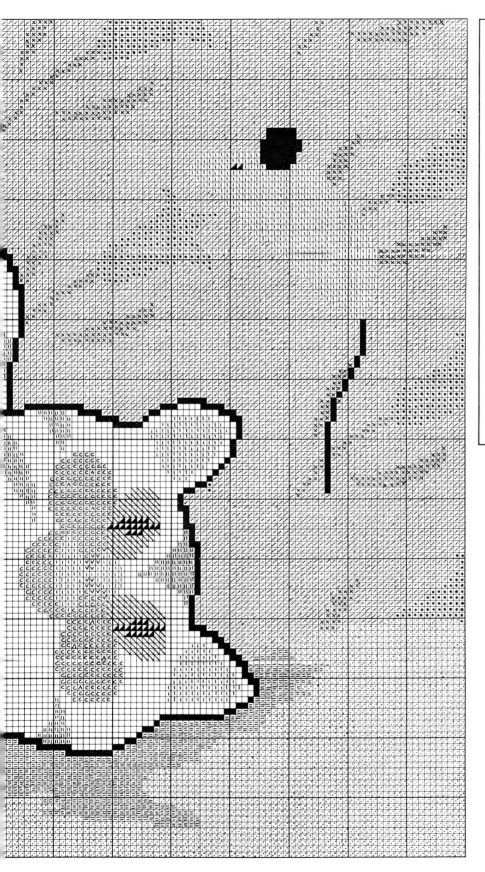

CARTOON CAT

Symbol	Code	Colour
╱	7313	Blue
☒	7345	Green
•	7606	Bright Red
■	7401	Light Brown
□	7078	Pale Yellow
C		White
‖	7846	Tan
⊟	7961	Dark Dusky Rose
⸪	7951	Dusky Rose
⊺	7192	Flesh Pink
◤		Black
△	7270	Pale Grey
∨	7215	Medium Flesh Pink
◹	7771	Pale Green

NEEDLEPOINT DOORSTOP

A simple but practical project that turns an ordinary builders' brick into an attractive and very effective doorstop. And it also makes an excellent starter if this is your first encounter with needlepoint. This design is based on a padded standard size brick, measuring 8 x 21 x 6cm (4¼ x 8¼ x 2¼in). However, bricks differ in size, so it is wise to check the measurements of your own brick, and adjust the design accordingly, if necessary.

MATERIALS

A piece of double-thread canvas with 10 stitches to the inch (2.5cm), 43cm (17in) deep x 51cm (20in) wide
A clean standard shape brick (see above)
50cm (½yd) smooth, heavy cotton fabric, 90cm (36in) wide
A piece of heavy felt, 13 x 24cm (5 x 9½in)
Small amount of wadding
Narrow masking tape
71 small round pearl beads
DMC tapestry wool in the colours indicated
DMC stranded cotton in Pearl Grey (415)
Dark grey and white sewing thread

1 Prepare your brick by placing some wadding in the frog indentation, holding it in place with two strips of masking tape. Then wrap the cotton fabric around the brick, securing it with masking tape or tacking stitches, so that it is smoothly and evenly padded all round.
2 Work your needlepoint in one piece as shown in the diagram. When completed, work the backstitch detail. Then sew on the beads, using white thread.
3 Cut away the excess canvas, allowing a 2.5cm (1in) border of unworked canvas all round. Fold this surplus canvas under to the wrong side.
4 Turn the work over and pin the short sides of the canvas together, so that it resembles a box-lid.

5 Using the same colour wool as the needlepoint in that area, sew together each two adjacent sides with a strong backstitch, making a seam which includes one worked row of stitches alongside the 2.5cm (1in) of unworked canvas. Sew all four corners together in the same way.
6 Turn the canvas to the right side and fit the cover over the brick. If necessary, add some more cotton padding to make the cover fit the brick more snugly.
7 When the fit has been satisfactorily adjusted, stitch the felt base into position. Turn in the edges of the felt about 5mm (¼in) on all sides before pinning it into place. Using dark grey thread, slip-stitch the felt one row deep into the needlepoint, making a neat finished edge.

Doorstop construction
diagram

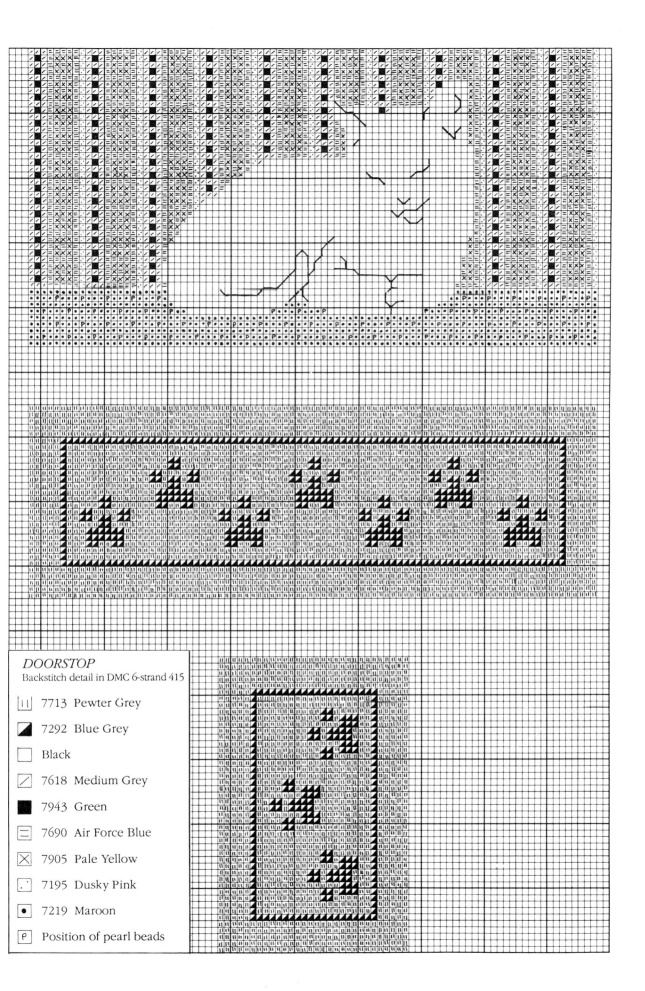

DOORSTOP
Backstitch detail in DMC 6-strand 415

Symbol	Code	Colour
⊔⊔	7713	Pewter Grey
◣	7292	Blue Grey
☐		Black
⟋	7618	Medium Grey
■	7943	Green
⩮	7690	Air Force Blue
⨯	7905	Pale Yellow
⠐	7195	Dusky Pink
●	7219	Maroon
P		Position of pearl beads

5
MINIATURE GIFTS

FRAMES, TRINKET BOXES AND PAPERWEIGHTS

In addition to the embroidery threads and wools used throughout this book, DMC also produce a range of paperweights, miniature frames and trinket boxes. These can be used to display your embroidery in a practical way. But they can also make attractive ornaments, mementoes and presents – just by mounting any attractive or personal picture inside.

Tasteful illustrations from old greetings cards can supply a wonderful selection of subjects, both artistic and endearing: anything from sprays of flowers to lovable bears! Religious subjects would appeal to many, whilst photographs of loved ones or family pets provide a specially personal touch, if you are looking for original presents for family and friends.

1 Place your miniature frame, paperweight or trinket box lid over the card, positioning it to the best advantage over the picture. Mark lightly all round the edge of the lid, using a sharp pencil.
2 Now use the template provided to mark round again, this time to give you the correct size for your cutting line.
3 Follow the manufacturer's instructions for making up the item.

FRAMED MINIATURES WALL HANGING

A novel, pretty – and inexpensive – way to display your miniature pictures. It is simple to do, and all you need is a length of ribbon or lace; a brass curtain ring; and a needle and matching thread.

1 Decide how many miniature frames you wish to display, then place them in a line, one above the other, on a flat surface. Consider the effect, and when you are happy with the spacing, measure the total length of the display, adding a few extra centimetres or inches at the top (as illustrated). Double this measurement (to allow for folding the ribbon or lace in half): this will give you the amount of ribbon/lace needed for your hanging.
2 Pass the ribbon/lace through the hanging ring of your bottom picture, folding it in half so that the frame is held in the fold.
3 Lay your other pictures on top of the double ribbon/lace, and mark with tailor's chalk where they will be positioned.
4 Starting at the bottom (your second picture up), make a row of tiny backstitches across the ribbon/lace and pass one piece of ribbon through the hanging ring so that the picture is held by the stitches. Continue in this way until all your pictures are in position.
5 Stitch the ends of the ribbon or lace together at the top, sewing in the curtain ring as you do so.

INDEX